Real-Life Wisdom

Real-Life Wisdom

◆

Stories for the Road

Bob Ayres

iUniverse, Inc.
New York Lincoln Shanghai

Real-Life Wisdom
Stories for the Road

iUniverse, Inc.

For information address:
iUniverse, Inc.
2021 Pine Lake Road, Suite 100
Lincoln, NE 68512
www.iuniverse.com

ISBN: 0-595-32595-5

Printed in the United States of America

Contents

Endorsements

"A rich blend of earthly expressions and Godly wisdom as he introduces us to good friends who made a difference; a great read for any Christian, but a must for those in relational ministry."

Bruce Baker, Executive Director
Bluegrass Youth for Christ
Lexington, Kentucky

"Relational Evangelism is meant to be impacting. While our focus has traditionally been on how well we relate to others, Bob Ayres invites a new perspective in appreciating how others relate to us and impacts us along our journey in life. Through *Real-Life Wisdom: Stories for the Road*, Bob masterfully combines life's most precarious moments with insight from both scripture and conventional wisdom to take me on a journey that I found myself thinking and reflecting on those who made an impact upon my life. This is excellent reflective material that invites us to be more involved. Bob not only challenges us to reflect, but also to share with the inclusion of his discussion starter guide at the end of the book. For anyone interested in light reading that sparks introspection, this is a must read."

Rev. Rick McClain, Deaf Pastor
College Church of the Nazarene
Olathe, Kansas

"Bob Ayres is one of the most sincere, honest and straightforward people I know. He is an impressive minister who can reach kids. His insight will definitely help you with your ministry."

Conway Stone
Author and Speaker

"It is evident that Bob is keenly aware of the many relationships in his life—intentional and unintentional. The amazing thing about *Real-Life Wisdom: Stories for the Road* is that others are now able to read about what many of us have known. It is more than those quotes and sayings that have impacted Bob's life. It is a handbook by which others may learn and apply principles to their lives. This book will always have a space on my bookshelf."

Rev. Logan Murphy, Minister of Recreation
Northeast Christian Church
Louisville, Kentucky

"Bob brings refreshing, candid, practical words of wisdom and insight into every day ministry. This is an honest, upbeat, positive and encouraging book that helped to renew and refocus my perspective as I go about the ministry that God has called me to. I kept thinking of all the folks that I wanted to share this book with! Read it—and you will be encouraged!"

Pam Moore, Regional Director
Young Life in the Pioneer Region
Omaha, Nebraska

"Real-Life Wisdom: Stories for the Road is a fun and fresh look at relational ministry. Bob Ayres teaches important lessons by introducing us to people he has met through out his life and sharing a glimpse of the truths he learned. This book is a very practical guide for anyone serving in today's culture."

Mary Tatum, Deaf and Disabilities Ministries
Southeast Christian Church
Louisville, Kentucky

"A really good book written by a real author with real quotes from real people with real experiences for real people interested in real relationships in a real world!"

Rev. Chad Entinger
Faribault, Minnesota

"I've found this book to be very enjoyable. I believe it is a source of wisdom from those who have had the life experiences, so that we can learn from it. I believe it will be an excellent tool for small groups. I look forward to the discussions it will generate."

John Gretz, Area Director
Young Life Oldham County
Crestwood, Kentucky

"Bob Ayres is one of my favorite people. I value his counsel, his insight and most of all his friendship. He has written a book that every pastor, and especially every 'would-be' pastor should read three times to really understand what it means to 'do' ministry the way Jesus would have us do it."

Steve Idle, Pastor of Membership
Northeast Christian Church
Louisville, Kentucky

PROVERBS 1

[1] The proverbs of Solomon son of David, king of Israel:

[2] for attaining wisdom and discipline; for understanding words of insight;

[3] for acquiring a disciplined and prudent life, doing what is right and just and fair;

[4] for giving prudence to the simple, knowledge and discretion to the young—

[5] let the wise listen and add to their learning, and let the discerning get guidance—

[6] for understanding proverbs and parables, the sayings and riddles of the wise.

[7] The fear of the Lord is the beginning of knowledge, but fools despise wisdom and discipline.

New International Version of the Bible

ABBREVIATIONS

NIV	New International Version of the Bible
NASB	New American Standard Bible
MSG	The Message
NLT	New Living Translation
CEV	Contemporary English Version
NKJV	New King James Version
ESV	English Standard Version

Introduction

"Originality is the art of forgetting where you heard something." I don't remember where I heard that…maybe I came up with it myself! No, actually, this is a quote from the late Dr. O. Dean Martin, at one time pastor of one of the fastest growing United Methodist churches in the country…now, I don't know where *he* got it.

In fact, it doesn't matter. If he didn't come up with it, chances are the person he heard it from didn't come up with it either. It reminds me of urban myths that go through various changes in many cultures but the basic story remains constant through centuries of use.

This book is unapologetically based on the quotes of people who have influenced my life. These are the words I have learned from wonderful people who have left their proverbial thumbprint on my forehead. As a husband, father, friend, and minister, I have quoted these and other words from time to time; maybe even more often than I care to admit. There is such incredible wisdom in simple words. I find them to be principles by which I make decisions. I start out each chapter with their name and something about the person from whom I learned the quote. These wonderful memories and sayings have given me such encouragement over the years. Maybe you can benefit as well.

A saying is like *the moral of the story.* It is a way to summarize an entire experience into a single phrase. I grew up with these types of pithy sayings. My mother has an Irish and Scottish heritage and has a saying for virtually any situation. If I wished for something, she would say, *"If wishes were horses, beggars would ride."* If I was ever tempted to leave behind my mark or initials, I would remember her warning, *"Fools names and fools faces, always seen in public places."* Something inexpensive that quickly fell apart was explained with, *"Well, you get what you pay for."* I assume every family has sayings that are rich with meaning and memory. I hope this book brings some to your mind.

Recently, I had the honor of meeting Dr. Charles W. Conn, a scholar and leader in the Church of God denomination based in Cleveland, Tennessee. He is the grandfather of David Cannon, a close friend and colleague of mine. Dr. Conn has published a number of historical and devotional books. As I was leaving his home, he handed me a couple of books as a gift. One of the books was *The Pointed Pen: The Maxims of Charles W. Conn* published by the Lee College Alumni Association in 1973. It is a small book of powerful sayings crafted by Dr. Conn. He describes a maxim as *"a small slice of truth in a fashion that is particularly illuminating."* His wisdom is so deep and timeless that I decided to sprinkle some of his 691 maxims across these pages. As the husband of one and the father of twelve (each who has also contributed greatly to our world), his words and wisdom add valuable seasoning to this book. I am grateful for his qualities and insights that endure through time.

All the scriptures in the context of the chapters are from the New International Version which I find to be a solid translation that is both readable and scholarly. I tried to use a variety of versions in the quotes from Proverbs for the purpose of exposing the reader to the wealth of translations now available. Proverbs 3:5-6 that carried me through some difficult days… *"Trust in the Lord with all your heart and lean not on your own understanding. In all your ways acknowledge Him and He will make your paths straight."* I praise God for the simplicity and truth of that scripture.

My appreciation goes out to Steve Idle, John Gretz, Logan Murphy, Linda Rueff, Larry and Sue Rueff, Ben Sharpton, and Kathy Ayres for reviewing the first draft and making solid recommendations for improvement. Dad, I treasure our weekly breakfasts together and the conversations we've shared. Mom, thanks for the colorful heritage full of laughter, creativity, and plenty of practical sayings. I thank you both for your love.

Make no mistake about it, my life will be judged by God primarily on how I loved and cared for my family. It is not the only important thing but I am convinced it makes up a major part of the final exam. Kathy, Christina, David, Casey, John, and Ana...you are the lights of my life as I struggle to serve the Light of Life. I praise God for you all!

This is a practical guide for relational ministry. Your ministry may be with your children, your spouse, your workplace, or as a volunteer or professional minister. In Bible school or seminary, you learn ancient languages and current trends; it is important to become well educated. But always remember to connect with the real world where you learn about the stuff of life. May your journey be exciting, challenging, and filled with the peace from God. May you give to others as Christ has given to you.

Bob Ayres

○ ○
"For the LORD gives wisdom, and from his mouth come knowledge and understanding."

—Proverbs 2:6 NIV

1

If we all switched chairs, this conversation would be completely different.

Tim Dobbins is the youth leader who first helped me connect to a personal relationship with Jesus Christ. Tim was an amazing young man and volunteer with an outreach ministry called Young Life. He was only twenty years old at the time (I was eighteen). Tim's charisma was spell-binding for me as a senior in high school. I began to walk, talk, laugh, and think like Tim Dobbins. This was at a time when my desire for individuality was at an all-time high. Tim was a kid-magnet mostly because of how he made you feel about yourself. You felt like Tim really liked you and respected what you had to say. He knew that the key to ministry (and life in general) is not trying to get people to like you, rather letting them know that you like them. This was part of the magic of his personality.

Tim often brought laughter to our group when he would quip, *"You know, if we all switched chairs, this conversation would be completely different."* I still smile when I think of this phrase. What in the world was he talking about? It took me awhile to make sense out of this. I thought Tim was just being funny. He was actually communicating an important truth that I would later discover for myself.

According to my father, who was a math professor, if you have five people in a meeting around a table, the potential number of combinations of where people are seated is a "Five factorial" or 5 x 4 x 3 x 2 x 1 = 120 different combinations. Each one would have its own distinct pattern of interaction. If you are in a meeting and things are not going well, maybe just ask everyone if they don't mind changing seats!

It makes me ask myself, *"How do I interact in groups?"* I notice that virtually every time I walk into a meeting, I check out the seating arrangement. I have become quite proficient at the skill of surveillance and strategy. I subtly decide on the best seat at the table to accomplish my personal goal. Is this wrong?

Sometimes, I intend to be an invisible member of the meeting. I simply want to stay beneath the radar screen, off the firing line. I want to avoid being stuck in the trenches. Carefully, I plot my words like an advisor to the general at military headquarters. I've prepared for battle and am running on stealth mode. Sounds like guerrilla warfare. Probably describes my state of mind in those meetings. Choose the seat least likely to draw attention to myself. My advantaged position is often silence followed by carefully crafted words.

At other times, I am determined to acquire the seat of power; seize and maintain through intellect and articulation. My goal is a specific outcome of the meeting. I may use humor, personal warmth or even gentle confrontation. I make sure my back is to the wall and the key players at the table are within eye contact and earshot. Chairs that are slightly elevated are best. Regardless of my agenda, I am almost always intentional about where I sit in a meeting. I do not want to be vulnerable. I want to operate from a perspective of control.

But somehow, the words of Jesus keep popping up in my head. He was keenly aware of where people sat at the table. He says we are to take the lesser seat; to avoid lording power over others. One time, Jesus confronted two brothers vying for positions of power. *"Jesus called them together and said, "You know that those who are regarded as rulers of the Gentiles lord it over them, and their high officials exercise authority over them. Not so with you. Instead, whoever wants to become great among you must be your servant, and whoever wants to be first must be slave of all."* (Mark 10:42-44)

What if we rearranged the seating at a table? Would the conversation be completely different? Do I apply this same principle to how I choose my clothing, what car I drive, who my friends are, where I live and work? Do I tend to put myself in an advantaged position? Does my being in an advantaged position put others in a disadvantaged position? Does my being an "insider" create "outsiders?"

If my position at the table was one of the uneducated working man, would I have a different perspective? If I were a woman at the table, would I find sexual innuendoes in the conversation to be charming or cute? If I were a person of color, would I understand the tenseness on the faces of the others in the room when I express a controversial opinion?

The beginning of knowledge is recognizing that which we have not experienced—of knowing where we haven't been or cannot go. This is part of the reason we pay close attention to those in other seats at the table.

How does it feel to be dying of cancer? What would it be like to have an adult child who is mentally handicapped? How hard is it to live with a spouse or child with mental illness? How difficult is life for those who are in prison or have a criminal record? What is it like to lose a child? What makes sense when nothing makes sense?

I have spent most of my adult life in ministry with people from whom I am different. Often referred to as "cross-cultural" ministry, this means I am an outsider in another culture. I am the one who is different. I am white, and have ministered with African-American youth. I am an adult and have entered the world of the adolescent. I worked on behalf of people with brain injury yet have not personally experienced this trauma. I am hearing and currently minister within the Deaf community. Make no mistake about it. If you are ministering in another culture, you are always a visitor, regardless of where you sit at the table.

The one thing we share in common, across all cultures, is our incredible need for connection with God and each other. The ground really is level at the foot of the cross. We are truly equals and equally in need of right relationships. Gather with those different from yourself. Approach them as equals who have more to teach you than you have to teach them. You are the visitor. Go with respect, humility, vulnerability; then God will use you.

Tim was right. If we switched chairs, this conversation would be completely different. Any meal-time discussion is best when Jesus is the honored guest at the table. We come together as brothers and sisters in Christ. Let's listen carefully to Jesus and to each another. Pay attention to the seating arrangement. Notice and respect the opinions of others at the table. You will learn a great deal from their life experiences. Humility is an essential building block for impacting the lives of others; for being a caring person. We have much to learn from each other.

◆   ◆   ◆

Where is he now? Tim Dobbins is the President of Leadership Technologies, Inc., and works as a leadership and communications consultant to business, government and not-for-profit organizations here and abroad. He is valued as a keynote speaker and corporate retreat leader. He designs conferences, leads seminars, lectures, and writes on cultural architecture, leadership development, executive coaching, conflict management, and organizational team building. He has been a guest lecturer at the Wharton School and is a Fellow of the British-American Project, affiliated with Johns Hopkins School for Advanced International Studies and The Royal Institute, London. He studied and taught in Jerusalem, the United Kingdom and Zurich. Tim is the author of Business Companion, a business phrase book translated into Chinese, Spanish, and German. He is also author of *"Making the Most of Change: Strategies for the Oval Office and Your Office"*-Random House.

> *The tailor should not covet the carpenter's nail, and the*
> *carpenter should not despise the tailor's needle.*
> Charles W. Conn

o o o o o o o o o o o o o o o o o o o o o o o o o o o o o o o

"My child, never forget the things I have taught you. Store my commands in your heart, for they will give you a long and satisfying life."

—Proverbs 3:1-2 NLT

2

Show up. Show up, dressed. Show up, dressed and ready to play.

Back when I was teaching middle and high school, a motivational speaker was brought in at the beginning of the school year to inspire the teachers. The entire faculty was gathered for a required training event in the middle school cafeteria. The speaker looked a bit like a used car salesman to me. His hair was black "from-a-bottle" and slicked back in a style common thirty years earlier. I was all attitude thinking, *"What a goofball. Why in the world do I have to sit here and listen to him?"* It was my first year of teaching and I had plenty of work waiting for me. I took my seat, slouched a bit and kept one eye on the clock.

Pride goes before the fall or in this instance, the autumn. This motivational speaker proclaimed one of the more significant things I've heard over the years and have used it as a foundation for facing many of my challenges in life. The first step in learning something new is recognizing the absence of prior knowledge. I was never very good at that first step. As I get older, humility comes more naturally to me.

He told the story of a conversation he had with a young man who approached him after he had given a previous motivational speech.

The young man asked, *"What do I need to do to be successful?"*

This sage thought for a moment and then responded plainly, "Show up."

There was a brief silence.

"What do you mean?"

"Just show up. That's all you need to do. You will have a delightful and successful life. People will appreciate you and acknowledge your contributions."

"*Okay...*" the young man nodded hesitantly. *"Just show up"* seemed like an odd response but *whatever.*

The speaker continued, "Now, if you *really* want to get ahead, receive accolades and have people remark about your impressive qualities, then...without a doubt, show up, *dressed.*"

"*Dressed?*"

"Yes, dressed. Not only clean and in pleasant attire but with your mind dressed. Your attitude dressed. Give attention to the details of how you present yourself. Be ready to perform."

The young man had an expression locked somewhere between incredulity and horror. These were not the answers he was pursuing. Certainly, there had to be more. *"You mean, that's all there is to it."*

"Oh, no. There's one more thing" the wise teacher continued.

"If you *REALLY* want to blow them away, take control, have buildings named after you, find yourself in positions of influence and power, then show up...dressed...and *ready to play.*"

"*Ready to play?*"

"Ready to play."

Silence.

"Show up *prepared.* Study the issue before the meeting. Think of alternatives and solutions before you walk in the door. Be ready to play; ready to present your ideas. Have your handouts printed and the master plan in your mind. If you will do this simple thing, you will control the world. That's about all there is to it. *Show up...*show up *dressed...*and be *ready to play.*"

I am now aware that this is an old football saying used to inspire young men at the first practice of the season but for me, it was new. *So, maybe I was late to football practice once or twice.* Besides, the speaker told the story as though it really happened. *Maybe it even actually did!*

The rest of his presentation faded into the recesses of my memory but his point was simple yet profound. I was so dull. I didn't really get it at first. My mind was busy and distracted. The wisdom of these words dawned on me over the next few months. Over the past twenty or so years, it has virtually become a mantra of mine.

There are times in my life that the best I can do is *show up*. Anyone who has raised children understands this adage. *Show up* for doctor's appointments. *Show up* for teacher conferences. *Show up* for housework. *Show up* for your spouse. *Show up* for dinner. *Show up* for conversations with your children. *Show up* and you will survive.

There are many ministry situations that are simply unpleasant. I have visited friends in jail and in hospitals and found myself repeating, *just show up*. Ministers who never put themselves in uncomfortable situations are not real ministers, they are entertainers. They only perform for appreciative crowds. It is amazing how important it is to show up in during the difficult times in people's lives. Don't let uncertainty paralyze you, respond. Start by simply *showing up*.

Secondly, be aware of how you present yourself. Show up, *dressed*. Have a positive attitude about the opportunity to love other people. God has given you a life full of hope. Share the wealth of abundant life. Meet people on their level. Be willing to adapt your appearance to fit the situation. This may mean wearing a nice outfit to a business lunch or jeans and a t-shirt when you are hanging out with teenagers. But it is much more than just what you wear, it is how you *dress* your mind; how you view the other person. See them as God sees them. Dress yourself in garments that allow you to see others through God's eyes. Look people in the eye even if they make you uncomfortable. Adorn yourself with respect for others. *Dress* yourself with class.

Finally, show up, dressed and *ready to play*. It takes a tremendous amount of planning to make something look spontaneous and fresh. The mark of a professional is someone who can accomplish incredible feats and make it look easy. This only happens because the professional was preparing while others were out wasting time. Study the situation before entering into it. Ask advice of others who have been there before. Prayer is a vital part of showing up *ready to play*. There is nothing magical about excellence. It is simply a matter of taking your responsibilities seriously enough to prepare. In Luke 14:28-29, Jesus spoke of the importance of estimating costs before beginning to build…show up *prepared*.

Jesus uses another story to warn about being unprepared. *"At that time the kingdom of heaven will be like ten virgins who took their lamps and went out to meet the bridegroom. Five of them were foolish and five were wise. The foolish ones took their lamps but did not take any oil with them. The wise, however, took oil in jars along with their lamps. The bridegroom was a long time in coming, and they all became drowsy and fell asleep. At midnight the cry rang out: 'Here's the bridegroom! Come out to meet him!' Then all the virgins woke up and trimmed their lamps. The foolish ones said to the wise, 'Give us some of your oil; our lamps are going out.' 'No,' they replied, 'there may not be enough for both us and you. Instead, go to those who sell oil and buy some for yourselves.' But while they were on their way to buy the oil, the bridegroom arrived. The virgins who were ready went in with him to the wedding banquet. And the door was shut." Matthew 25:1-10*

Are you a caring person? Do you want to have the full impact on the lives of others? Do you want to be an effective minister? Do you want your life to "make a difference in this world?"

Show up.

Show up *dressed*.

Show up dressed and *ready to play*.

Fame is sometimes accidental, but greatness never is.
Charles W. Conn

o o o o o o o o o o o o o o o o o o o o o o o o o o o o o o o

"Trust in the LORD with all your heart and do not lean on your own understanding; in all your ways acknowledge him, and he will make your paths straight."

—*Proverbs 3:5-6 NASB*

3

God is with you through the darkness.

Robin Groth and I were best friends in high school. We started a folk music group (okay, so I'm showing my age) and wrote all our own music. We called ourselves *Horizon*. Neither of us had an understanding of a personal relationship with God at this point but even the name of the group spoke about what was to come; hope for a new day. Our music reflected a quest for truth and meaning in life. There was a longing in our hearts for a connection with God.

Robin knew me at my loneliest time. I was not a Christian when we first became friends. Her laughter brought light into my world. She has bright, blue eyes and natural blond hair that reflects her German heritage. She has a wonderful, quick laugh and accomplished musical skills. We spent many hours together dreaming of Colorado and adventures in the world of performing music.

Robin and I never dated. There was nothing romantic about our relationship, only a warm and abiding friendship. We stopped playing music together during my senior year of high school and drifted apart. I was busy with school and work and dating. We both moved on to other interests and lost touch.

During my senior year of high school, I became a Christian. Through relationships with Christian adults who loved me in spite of my faults, I was able to make sense of God's incredible grace. It was a process that took a few months but at some point I realized that if God loved me that much, I could learn to love myself. I accepted the abundance of the love of the one who created me.

After high school, I became a volunteer leader with a youth ministry program. I was a young Christian. It was an exciting time of growing and learning each day what it means to follow Jesus Christ. God was doing a major renovation of my mind and spirit. I slept little and often carried on deep discussions into the early morning hours over coffee and cheesecake.

One time, late in the evening, I was at a party at a friend's house when I received a call. It was from Robin. We had not talked for almost two years. I answered the phone in a noisy living room. I had to close my eyes and plug my other ear to understand her quiet voice on the phone.

"Are you busy?" She said.

"No," I fibbed. "What's up?"

"I just need to talk with someone. I didn't know who to call. Can we meet somewhere?"

"Sure."

We picked a local 24-hour restaurant. I arrived first and selected a table in a vacant section in the back. We hugged as she reached the table and it was great to see each other. It had been a long time since we were together. We ordered a pot of coffee and dessert.

I remember enjoying a great conversation about a number of things but there seemed to be nothing specific on the agenda. She knew I had accepted Christ and was interested in how this impacted my life. We chatted. I told her about my personal experience with Jesus Christ and the new hope I found. I simply opened my heart and shared about my experience. A few hours later, we hugged again and went our separate ways. I quietly wondered why she phoned me, late at night, and called me away from a party for a somewhat casual conversation.

I later learned it was a matter of life and death.

It was an extremely fragile time in her life that night and my name kept coming up in her mind. I still don't know how she got the number for my friend's house. I'm glad she did. Our conversation gave her hope. Robin soon became a follower of Jesus Christ. She later told me that her deal with God was, *if you are real, let there be someone who shows that they care.* Completely unaware, I simply showed up.

Three weeks after accepting Jesus into her life as Lord and Savior, Robin was confronted with a terrible crisis. Her father, step-mother, little sister, and their baby-sitter were all killed in a car crash. The news was an incredible shock.

Robin's relationship with her father had been estranged; it was in the initial process of being rekindled. Suddenly, he was gone. Three weeks after becoming a Christian, she was slammed with the reality that horrific things sometimes happen to good people. Life can become unbelievably painful. People die; the hurt lives on.

How did Robin respond?

She could have totally rejected the God of the universe for the tragedy that so closely followed her conversion but she didn't. She drew near. She let the One who knew ultimate sorrow, draw her closely and hold her. There was no hint of trying to explain away the shock and grief. Robin knew that sometimes bad things happen in life. Sometimes, there is no logic that can make sense of the illogical...but always, God is with us.

"When Jesus spoke again to the people, he said, 'I am the light of the world. Whoever follows me will never walk in darkness, but will have the light of life.'" (John 8:12) Jesus later comforted his disciples with these words. *"Do not let your hearts be troubled. Trust in God; trust also in me." (John 14:1)*

One cannot turn bad things into good things by simply attributing them to God. Bad things are bad things. God can use even bad experiences to bring about good things but this doesn't change the reality of evil. Ultimately God wins but remember he is not the only player on the field. There is another who is the author of brokenness. The good news is that we are not alone as we face crises. God wins.

She held the nail-scarred hand as she stood before the tomb.

Life would never be the same.
But she was never alone.

Robin became a volunteer leader with the youth ministry program. We worked closely together over the next number of years. She is a strong, loving, fun, woman of God who brings character and kindness to her ministry. She understands pain. She also understands the comfort that only a relationship with the Creator brings.

Isaiah 53:3 refers to the Messiah as *a "man of sorrows, and familiar with suffering."* The writer of Hebrew defines our Lord as one who faced every temptation; even the temptation we experience to turn our backs on God when life gets too painful. Yet, Jesus never sinned. *"Therefore, since we have a great high priest who has gone through the heavens, Jesus the Son of God, let us hold firmly to the faith we profess. For we do not have a high priest who is unable to sympathize with our weaknesses, but we have one who has been tempted in every way, just as we are—yet was without sin. Let us then approach the throne of grace with confidence, so that we may receive mercy and find grace to help us in our time of need."* Hebrew 4:14-16.

Robin found mercy and grace in her time of need. She found comfort. She made it through the dark days and has the strength to face more. She is now a social work counselor; a mentor and friend to many. She can empathize with other's pain. She, too, has walked through the valley of the shadow of death. She is no stranger to loss. She is also familiar with hope that comes only from knowing you are loved, with the deepest love, by the Creator of the Universe. Life has meaning, even in darkness, when we realize that great love God has for us. Psalm 17:8 says, *"Keep me as the apple of your eye; hide me in the shadow of your wings."* Our worth comes from knowing God believes we are worthy.

Robin always wanted to live out west. Three years after we graduated from high school, I helped her jam all her things into my yellow, Volkswagen beetle and drove her across the country to deliver her to the land of her dreams. She got to live in her Colorado Rocky Mountains.

People have different ways to try to make sense out of tragedy. Some may try to give comfort by attributing evil events to a loving God. They may hide behind religion. *"God's ways are mysterious. We cannot understand why God has done this."* God calls us into relationship, not religion. I personally believe this perspective of God as the author of evil sets people up for a crisis of faith. It may give temporary relief but plants the seeds of deep doubts as to the very nature and existence of God. I think it is much healthier to accept the reality of our broken world and recognize that God will never leave us or forsake us. He is our Comforter. He gives, *"the peace of God, which transcends all understanding, will guard your hearts and your minds in Christ Jesus." (Philippians 4:7)* This is all that we need.

Shortly before his death, Jesus sat at the table with his closest friends and whispered these words, *"Peace, I leave with you. My peace I give to you; not as the world gives, do I give to you. Let not your heart be troubled, nor let it be fearful." (John 14:27)*

Robin has been there and she knows.

Do not be afraid.

God is with you through the darkness.

◆   ◆   ◆

Where is she now? Robin Groth Miller lives in Missoula, Montana with her husband, Theron. She has a Masters in Counseling; having worked twenty years as a therapist, the last fourteen years at the Mental Health Center in Missoula working with Adults diagnosed with serious mental illnesses. Her hobbies include backpacking, hiking, cross country skiing, rafting, travel, reading, and being outdoors. Robin and Theron celebrated their 20th wedding anniversary by taking a trip to Norway—A far different trip than their honeymoon when they took a two-month bicycle trip from Seattle to Alaska. Robin's favorite scripture is Philippians 3:12-17, *"Not that I have already obtained all this, or have already been made perfect, but I press on to take hold of that for which Christ*

Jesus took hold of me. Brothers, I do not consider myself yet to have taken hold of it. But one thing I do: Forgetting what is behind and straining toward what is ahead, I press on toward the goal to win the prize for which God has called me heavenward in Christ Jesus. All of us who are mature should take such a view of things. And if on some point you think differently, that too God will make clear to you. Only let us live up to what we have already attained. Join with others in following my example, brothers, and take note of those who live according to the pattern we gave you." Her favorite bumper sticker is *"The Best Form of Revenge is Living Well."*

God will hear the cry of His children from afar, but we should live so close to Him that He can hear our faintest whisper of prayer.

Tears are the prisms that make rainbows in the soul.
Charles W. Conn

o o o o o o o o o o o o o o o o o o o o o o o o o o o o o o o o

"Do not be wise in your own eyes; Fear the LORD and depart from evil. It will be health to your flesh, and strength to your bones."

—*Proverbs 3:7-8 NKJV*

4

We'll try anything once.

Sarah was a REALLY old lady at our church. I met her when I was a young man; in fact, I am *still* not her age. She had snow-white hair, lots of wrinkles, and walked slowly. Yet, if she is to be judged by what I heard her say following a church meeting once, I believe she had the heart of an eighteen year-old.

The church was struggling with how to reach more people for Christ in the neighborhood. We were located in a part of town that was not exactly declining but was certainly not growing. Most of the neighborhood consisted of older people, transient renters, and a smattering of students attending the local university. The challenges for church growth were significant.

During a quarterly business meeting, different ideas were shared about new ministries to reach out to the community. Suggestions were floated and creativity was generally appreciated. No one knew exactly what to do but there was a general openness to new ideas. Leaving the meeting, I overheard Sarah say confidently to one of her friends about one of the ideas presented, *"Let's do it. We'll try anything once."*

Quite shocking coming from an old lady.

Sarah expressed what all effective ministers know; what matters is *attitude*. She was old and wise enough to have seen the danger inherent in being afraid to try. She oozed wisdom and experience. She probably went to grade school with some of the Apostles. She knew the value of being willing to take a risk and she wasn't afraid to try.

Her passion was for people to know God; this drives away all fear.

At the time, I was a Youth Minister at the church. I drove a motorcycle, wore jeans, a bandana, long hair and a beard–those things were actually *cool* back then. We took many risks with the program. We began a coffee house ministry on Friday nights as an outreach to local teens. I led a discipleship class for teenagers at six on Friday mornings (believe it or not, it was well attended). We programmed exciting events and camps. We were very intentional about building a team of committed adult leaders who took responsibility for relational ministry with teenagers. It was an exciting ministry.

ALL of these things are risky. We might *fail*. We might attract teenagers who didn't know how to *behave* in church. Someone may get *hurt*. Teenagers may bring *drugs* or *alcohol* into the mix. But as Sarah knew, the greatest risk was to play it safe. It is much riskier NOT to take risks. We must be willing to try anything once–in our efforts to introduce people to the person of Jesus Christ.

Be willing to try new ideas to reach different groups of people. Insanity has been defined as trying the same old thing and expecting a different result. Be willing to re-package the product to attract a new audience but keep the content consistent.

New wine deserves new wineskins. *"And no one pours new wine into old wineskins. If he does, the wine will burst the skins, and both the wine and the wineskins will be ruined. No, he pours new wine into new wineskins." (Mark 2:22)*

Jesus said he came to give us life, and give it abundantly. Pour it over, splash it around, dripping, and enjoy that refreshing life that wells up inside your heart. It is the passion of Jesus poured into our earthly vessels. Embrace the thrill of a new challenge. God took the ultimate risk when he sent Jesus into the world. He knew we may reject him. Many did. Many still do. He was willing to take the risk because of His love.

Remember the parable of the talents recorded in Matthew 25:24-26. *"Then the man who had received the one talent came. 'Master,' he said, 'I knew that you are a hard man, harvesting where you have not sown and gathering where you have not scattered seed. So I was afraid and went out and hid your talent in the ground. See, here is what belongs to you.'* *"His master replied, 'You wicked, lazy servant!"* The words of the Master become even harsher as the story continues. It is not a happy day for the servant who was afraid to try; afraid to risk, afraid to fail.

There is certainly a risk in taking risks. This is why it is called risky. It is easy to be fooled into believing something is right, just because it involves the thrill of risk-taking. Abundant life is fun and exciting and sometimes, risky. Sin provides a shadowy imitation of the thrill of abundant life. It is a deceptive mimic. That is the attraction of sin; taking risks is inherently exciting. We must avoid the trap of sin. Don't take risks simply for the thrill of taking them; have a calculated reason for your decisions. Be wise.

I am proud to say that I have failed at more things than most people have even thought of trying. I could wallpaper my office with rejection letters. It is no fun to fail but occasionally, something I have attempted has continued, and even flourished. This sure makes it fun. Above all, following Christ is about faithfulness, not success.

Start with a vision of what God wants to do in a particular situation. Put together a plan. Build consensus among like-minded people. Generate excitement. Give it a go. Be willing to fail. Be prepared to succeed. Many times you can solve an old problem with a new approach. If you fail, you'll be in the same place you are now, no real loss...except, hopefully...you will have learned a thing or two.

My wife and I have applied every bit of creativity, problem-solving skills, and risk-taking imaginable to raise our children to become decent human beings. Some thought it risky for us to adopt older children; they come with baggage. From what I've seen, those who birth their own children share a comparable risk. Children do not come with guarantees. We all make good and bad choices in life. The problem is people tend to be so human. It is risky business to start a family, yet God calls each generation to do so. We cannot be driven by fear. *"There is no fear in love. But perfect love drives out fear, because fear has to do with punishment. The one who fears is not made perfect in love." (1 John 4:18)*

If you are not living on the edge of potential failure, you are not living the abundant life. Even really old followers of Jesus know the importance of a good adventure. Be willing to try anything once. Who knows, it just may work. And if not, you are still in good company.

Fear sees a possibility and mistakes it for a problem;
faith sees a problem and recognizes it as an opportunity.
Charles W. Conn

o o o o o o o o o o o o o o o o o o o o o o o o o o o o o

"By wisdom the LORD laid the earth's foundations, by understanding he set the heavens in place; by his knowledge the deeps were divided, and the clouds let drop the dew. My son, preserve sound judgment and discernment, do not let them out of your sight; they will be life for you, an ornament to grace your neck. Then you will go on your way in safety, and your foot will not stumble; when you lie down, you will not be afraid; when you lie down, your sleep will be sweet."

—Proverbs 3:19-24 NIV

5

What will it matter in 100 years?

Dave Millhouser was my first youth leader when I was a sophomore in high school. What I remember about Dave is that he played Lacrosse, had a bizarre sense of humor, and seemed to like me as an individual. Dave was *wild and crazy* and full of abundant life. I always thought Christians were boring people. Dave's unique personality got my attention.

Dave was raised Jewish and became a Christian somewhere along the way. He taught me about the grace of God through Jesus Christ. This may seem a bit odd but Dave, steeped in his Jewish heritage, helped me rethink my tendency to try to earn my way into heaven. I find a certain irony and humor in this fact that a Jew was teaching a peripheral Protestant about grace. I guess it makes sense. Jesus was Jewish and he certainly understood God's love as a gift.

I didn't realize it at the time but Dave was modeling something I would learn to call relational ministry. It is the simple model Jesus showed us in loving people like God loves them…just because they are his creation. This is vital in earning the right to share the most important message in the world.

For a long time, I called this unconditional love. However, I think the word *unconditional* was more a product of the philosophies rampant during the late 1960's and early 1970's than it is an accurate expression of the scriptures. God's love may be *unmerited* or *unearned* or *undeserved* or *un-understood* (that should be a word) but it is not truly *unconditional*. There is one HUGE condition. We have to be willing to receive it.

I think *unconditional love* is supposed to mean *no matter what you've done or will do, God will still love you*. This is scriptural but as I get older, even this is a stretch for me. God's love for us *cannot* be erased or thwarted by our choices. There may be direct consequences, even eternal separation, but his love is *unchanging*. At best, I simply cannot fathom the fullness of the love of God. His love is powerful and present.

We have a saying that we have used with our children. *"Our love for you is stronger than your anger (or pain)."* Sometimes, their behavior was despicable, even violent. We could love them longer than they could behave horribly. It is not within their power to cause us to stop loving them. Love wins; hate (or hurt) loses. I guess this is what unconditional love means. God's love is more *enduring* than our sin. Wow.

Dave Millhouser taught me something else about grace. He had a saying that I have enjoyed repeating over the years, *"What will it matter in 100 years?"*

"What? What do you mean?" I responded when I first heard this.

He smiled. *"Really! These little things you are worried about, what will they matter in 100 years? Even 10 years. Most of the things you worry about today, won't even matter in a few months."*

"Okay…" I thought that was a little weird. As a high schooler, I could only envision about the next ten minutes.

"Worry about those things that really WILL matter in 100 years. The other things will probably take care of themselves."

That is really good advice…at any age.

As an adult, I find myself obsessing on paying bills, driving kids, running errands, dealing with homework, worrying about issues in the community or church, and being deeply concerned about national and international issues. How many of these things will matter in 100 years? Be concerned only about those that *will* matter in 100 years.

One of our local television stations will go anywhere in the world to find bad news. They are not satisfied with local tragedy, they pursue national and international calamity with a passion. If local news is not disturbing enough, they'll import pain. They want to be sure parents go to bed every night nervous about some potential threat to their families. They profit when we worry.

There are people who make entertainment out of obsessive worrying. Maybe this is part of the attraction of reality television. We don't have enough to worry about in our daily lives so we want to watch real people under stress. I tease my mother about worrying about things twice; once before it happens and then again, afterwards. Once is enough. Wait and see if something goes wrong and then worry. What you'll find is, by far, most of the time the tragedy never occurs. Don't borrow trouble from the future.

Jesus addresses worry in the Sermon on the Mount. *"Therefore I tell you, do not worry about your life, what you will eat or drink; or about your body, what you will wear. Is not life more important than food, and the body more important than clothes? Look at the birds of the air; they do not sow or reap or store away in barns, and yet your heavenly Father feeds them. Are you not much more valuable than they? Who of you by worrying can add a single hour to his life? So do not worry, saying, 'What shall we eat?' or 'What shall we drink?' or 'What shall we wear?' For the pagans run after all these things, and your heavenly Father knows that you need them. But seek first his kingdom and his righteousness, and all these things will be given to you as well. Therefore do not worry about tomorrow, for tomorrow will worry about itself. Each day has enough trouble of its own."* (Matthew 6:25-27, 31-34)

Worry is only one of the demons that will rob happiness. Don't forget anger, resentment, grief, regret, guilt, lust, prejudice, hate, and pride. You may want to ask yourself this question when tempted by any of these monsters, *"What WILL matter in 100 years?"* Think about the list of things you have worried about over the past twenty-four hours. How many concerns will still be pressing in even one year? How many concerns are so critical that you will still be worrying about them in even five years?

Works (as opposed to Grace) and *Worry* (as opposed to Peace) are joined at the hip. Part of Dave's message to me was *you worry because you are trying to control life; you are trying to earn your way into heaven. Give up what you cannot control to receive that which you cannot earn. Relax and enjoy to grace of God.*

How many things that concern us have life-long or even eternal consequences? In your heart, you already know the answers. These are the things that are really important today. Our sin will matter. The decisions we make now will affect generations to come. If you are facing temptation, flee! No sin is truly private; we are all connected. This is particularly true within families…and in churches.

Our families will matter. Most of the people I wanted to impress in my life have evaporated from my memory; I cannot even remember their names. I am confident most have no memory of me, either. But my children will remember me. My wife will remember me. My siblings, parents, relatives will all know I have been a part of their worlds. For better or worse (depending on the choices I make), they will remember my influence in their lives.

Redemption will matter. We are part of something much greater than ourselves. We are a small part of a larger plan to bring redemption to the world. God has called each one of us to use our talents for his glory. Most of us will be dead in 100 years. This is important. Being in a personal relationship with God through Jesus Christ will matter, eternally, for all of us.

Why do we tend to obsess on the minor and ignore the major? Jesus describes in Matthew 23:24, people who, *"…strain out a gnat but swallow a camel."* We choke on insignificant things and swallow some serious errors. We need to swallow the gnats in life that cause us such daily stress. We need to lay off the camel meat. It can be deadly.

Focus on what is truly important. Next time you are obsessing on some crisis that seems so large, so important, impossible to stop dwelling on, ask yourself…

"What will it matter in 100 years?"

♦   ♦   ♦

Where is he now? Dave Millhouser sent me this bio on himself. It was too good to edit. Here it is as he sent it…"Recently named as the official Poet Laureates of *Marine Services*, a New England based salvage firm, Dave and Sue Millhouser are underwater photographer/free lance writers living and working in New England. They were selected as *Artists in Residence of Cape Ann Divers* by a manager unfamiliar with the difference between "Artistic" and "Autistic." Their photographs and articles on North Atlantic marine life, dive sites and wrecks have appeared in a number of national magazines, including (honest) *Alert Diver, Scuba Times, Discover Diving, Rodale's Scuba Diving, Skin Diver, Sport Diver, Underwater USA, Sources, The Dive Journal*…and (in the pinnacle of their career) *National Bus Trader*. If you pay attention…you'll note that several of these are defunct. Having done slide presentations at *Beneath the Sea, The Boston Sea Rovers, Dive Philadelphia, Chicago's Our World Underwater* and the basement of the *Gloucester Public Library*…Just once they'd like to be invited someplace warm in the winter. In real life Dave is a cherubic bus salesman (whose favorite saying, oft repeated to customers, is *"I'm behind you 10%"*) and Sue is a right-wing Social Worker. While not in *Who's Who*, both are in *What's THAT?"*

Don't kill today by worrying it to death over tomorrow.
Charles W. Conn

o o o o o o o o o o o o o o o o o o o o o o o o o o o o o o
"Be wise and learn good sense; remember my teachings and do what I say. If you love Wisdom and don't reject her, she will watch over you. The best thing about Wisdom is Wisdom herself; good sense is more important than anything else. If you value Wisdom and hold tightly to her, great honors will be yours. It will be like wearing a glorious crown of beautiful flowers.

—Proverbs 4:5-9 CEV

6

Sometimes you only have two choices, both wrong.

Ken Casey is my brother-in-law and a good friend. We met in the eighth grade on the basketball court and became friends after high school. Ken and I lived together for a couple of years during college until Kathy and I got married. On the morning of my wedding, Ken and another roommate thought it would be hilarious to lock me in the bathroom. They tied a rope to the bathroom doorknob and secured it to another doorknob across the hallway. With their impressive knot-tying skills, escape was virtually impossible. At first, I thought it was a charming tease from a future brother-in-law however the confinement went on and on…lasting a couple of hours. It became less and less humorous as the time for the wedding drew near. I guess Ken finally accepted the idea of my joining his family so finally (barely in time to get to the church) he untied the ropes so I could escape my confinement in the bathroom. I was quite shocked to learn they had tape recorded my comments throughout the whole incident. Fortunately, I did not receive a blackmail note demanding money in exchange for the recording. I would have paid a handsome sum for that tape! For some reason my repeated and impassioned pleas, *"Come on, guys. This isn't funny!"* struck them as funny indeed!

Ken always loved philosophy and history. After a Master of Divinity at seminary, he earned his Ph.D. from Vanderbilt in Philosophy. At the same time, Ken maintains an earthy connection with bluegrass music; he plays guitar and banjo. He is an interesting mix of St. Augustine and Doc Watson. Talking to Ken is like reading the great writings of the early Church Fathers…published in *Mother Earth News*.

When we were young men, Ken and I were discussing age-old questions about right and wrong. *"If someone breaks into your house and you have only two choices, kill this person or they will murder your family, is it wrong to kill the intruder?"*

I figured the killing would be justified because of the reason behind it.

"No," Ken said. *"It's still wrong to kill."*

"But the other option is wrong, too!" I countered.

"True. But sometimes, you only have two options, and they're both wrong."

I was puzzled.

"Why would it be wrong? Isn't it right to prevent a greater wrong?"

Ken responded, *"The situation doesn't change right and wrong. It is still wrong to murder, although it may be preferable of the two bad choices. You may boldly and with conviction make the choice, knowing all along that it is clearly wrong."*

Not bad, Kenny.

This makes a great deal of sense. When you stand before God, you will still need to ask forgiveness for doing what was wrong, even if the other choice was even worse. You don't have the power to change the rules. Recognize when you have violated his law and ask for forgiveness. He already knows the situation.

It is never right to break the commandments God has given us. As a society, we may pass laws but we cannot legislate truth. If something proves to be untrue, it never was true. If it is indeed true, it always will be. Popular opinions, mores, folkways, and even cultures come and go…but ultimate truth is unchanging. We need God's forgiveness and healing. It is tempting to rationalize bad decisions but our explanations ring hollow; even if we only had two wrong choices to choose between. Don't try to justify mistakes; confess them to the loving God.

As a parent, I am MUCH more forgiving of a humble and contrite child than I am impressed by words of explanation. My primary agenda is my children's safety and ability to learn from mistakes by acknowledging, and ultimately, benefiting from the experience. We all make mistakes. I can live with that.

"If we say we have no sin, we are only fooling ourselves and refusing to accept the truth. But if we confess our sins to him, he is faithful and just to forgive us and to cleanse us from every wrong. If we claim we have not sinned, we are calling God a liar and showing that his word has no place in our hearts." (1 John 1:8-10)

I hate sin. I hate what sin does to people. I hate how it deceives and destroys. God's grace is about *redemption*, not tolerance or intolerance. It is about truth and love and hope. We must share the overwhelming love of Jesus Christ that calls all people into right relationships. It is a beckoning to the light of the world.

In reality, we almost always have more than two choices. Rarely are we in a "kill or be killed" situation. Actively look for other options. Seek the advice of those who've made plenty of mistakes. Be creative. Identify what the core problem is and focus on viable solutions.

In decision-making, there are six basic steps.

1) Identify the problem or core issue

2) Gather information about how others have addressed the problem

3) Come up with a variety of solutions

4) Determine the best solution from the list

5) Make a decision and act on this decision

6) Evaluate whether this solution worked; if not, start over.

Making a decision and *acting* on this decision is the *fifth* step. Have you adequately completed the first *four* steps before acting? To decide and *not act* is the same as *not deciding*. The key is being intentional in your effort to address the situation.

Occasionally, people will ask you to endorse immoral behavior based on the situation. They may seek your approval. Because you are a Christian and especially if you are a minister, they believe, *if YOU think something is right then it must be okay* and they feel their conscience is relieved. They justify bad choices by comparing them with worse options. They want your approval. I learned a long time ago that "judge not" means you are not in a position to determine someone's guilt…but you also cannot proclaim their innocence. You are not the judge, either way. You can point them to answers given in scripture. Speak the truth in love.

There have been times in my ministry where I said, in effect, *"If you are looking for me to give approval to your decision, it will never happen. I love you and will be there for you but I cannot lie and say I think this is good. All I can do is be a friend."*

Why is this important to you as a person trying to help others? Sometimes life does not give you a right and wrong choice, only the lesser of two evils. Realize that wrong is still wrong even for the right reasons. People need to take responsibility for their decisions…and be willing to accept forgiveness and healing.

"Then we will no longer be infants, tossed back and forth by the waves, and blown here and there by every wind of teaching and by the cunning and craftiness of men in their deceitful scheming. Instead, speaking the truth in love, we will in all things grow up into him who is the Head, that is, Christ." (Ephesians 4:14-15)

Sometimes in life you are stuck between two choices, both wrong. Don't try to justify yourself or explain anything or make excuses. Accept the reality of the situation and depend on the grace of God in Jesus Christ. This is the meaning of sinning boldly. Don't make decisions by indecision. Make a choice, even if it is wrong, and accept the consequences. Stand before God with honesty, integrity, and humility. Whenever possible, avoid putting yourself in these crisis situations. Save your energy for crises that you truly have no control over creating. There is enough evil in the world that you do not have to go looking for trouble. It will find you all on its own.

Confession…forgiveness…cleansing…healing…

There are some choices that are always right.

◆   ◆   ◆

Where is he now? Ken Casey lives in Bowling Green, Kentucky with his wife, Jane Olmstead and their sons, Galen, Adrian, and Casey. He teaches philosophy on a college level and has his Ph.D. from Vanderbilt University and his Master of Divinity from SBTS in Louisville, Kentucky. Ken plays and listens to bluegrass music. They have three dogs, a few cats and uncounted goldfish in the pond.

Like any good philosopher, Ken has a few favorite quotes from the ages… *"The unexamined life is not worth living"* (Socrates) *and "Thou hast made us for thyself, O Lord and our hearts are restless til they find their rest in thee."* (St. Augustine.) His favorite scripture is Phillipians 2:5-11, *"Have this mind in you which was also in Christ, who though he was in the form of God, did not count equality with God a thing to grasped, but instead emptied himself, taking the form of a servant, being born in the likeness of men. and being found in human form he humbled himself and become obedient unto death even death on a cross. Therefore God has exalted him and given him a name which is above every name, that at the name of Jesus every knee should bow, in heaven and on earth and under the earth and every tongue confess that Jesus Christ is Lord, to the glory of God the Father."*

Faith is like the roots of a tree, with knowledge as its branches. The greater and more luxuriant the branches become, the deeper the roots need to be; else, when the storms of doubt push against the branches, the tree will fall for lack of depth and strength.

Charles W. Conn

o o o o o o o o o o o o o o o o o o o o o o o o o o o o o o o

"Keep vigilant watch over your heart; that's where life starts. Don't talk out of both sides of your mouth; avoid careless banter, white lies, and gossip. Keep your eyes straight ahead; ignore all sideshow distractions."

—*Proverbs 4:23-25 MSG*

7

Never pet a wounded dog.

Alan Ayers is my older brother and a great friend. We were close enough in age to play together as youngsters yet he was old enough to become somewhat "larger than life" to me. He did things I only dreamed of like jumping out of planes and exploring haunted farmhouses. One of Alan's notable childhood accomplishments was the launching of numerous homemade hot air balloons created from plastic bags used to cover clothes from dry cleaners, a cross-bar of balsa wood and a bowl formed out of aluminum foil filled with burning alcohol. Many UFO sightings of the early 1970's could be credited to my brother. Besides being a scientist-in-training, he is the comedian of the family and a professional illustrator of book covers for a number of major publishers. He has an artistic talent for finding the humor or humorous irony in almost any situation. My oldest brother, younger sister and I usually provided the hysterical audience that could barely control our laughter when confronted with his antics.

Humor is a survival skill. We grew up in a less than perfect environment. We have wonderful parents who are much better apart than together. We also were a family slammed by alcoholism. In the midst of struggle, all of us, including my parents, maintained a great sense of humor. Laughter is a gift from God to give encouragement to the weary. Growing up, for me, was exhausting at times. I'm glad we always had laughter as a colleague and comforter.

One time, Alan was extremely upset about some incident–I cannot remember what–he was furious. Being the assigned peacemaker in the family, I felt it was my duty to rush in and comfort him. I knew my role. I had to help.

At that moment, my efforts to go talk to him and offer comfort were met with a harsh rebuke…this means he yelled something at me like, *"Go away! Leave me alone!"*

I was crushed. Tears welled up in my eyes. I was only trying to help. Why was he angry at me? Being the great brother he is, he calmed himself enough to share with me some wisdom that has served me well over the years.

He said, *"Never pet a wounded dog."*

One of the occupational hazards of ministers is the propensity for petting wounded dogs…and getting bitten. They don't necessarily want to bite you; you just rushed in too early. They were still in the "fight or flight" mode and you were foolish enough to reach out and touch. *Snap! Ouch!* Give people time when they are in the midst of a crisis. Show them this respect. Don't rush in.

My dad passed along another saying that was common lingo on the farm where he grew up: *"You'll draw back a nub!"* (It took me years to figure out this one.) It simply means, if you're not careful around farm machinery, you'll reach into something with an arm and pull back only a nub of what used to be your arm. It will change your life to stick your hand into some situations.

Let see… *"Never pet a wounded dog or you may draw back a nub."*

It seems people involved with relational ministry have a knack for rushing in. A compassionate heart and a quick reaction may combine for an impulsive response. Slow down. Don't just rush in to every dog fight. Pay attention for the right time to offer healing and friendship. I'm not talking about neglecting your duties to visit those in pain. Always show up! Just consider the variables when deciding when and how. You don't want to become part of the problem; no matter how well intentioned you may be.

One time I was leading a ministry team that had a terrible tension developing between two leaders. I was young and well-intentioned and lost my objectivity. My desire to fix the problem became part of the meltdown. It was an explosive situation that destroyed the unity of the team. This might have happened anyway but I made it worse by wading into the middle of the problem.

More recently, I had a similar situation where I moved more slowly and intentionally. I kept the responsibility on them to behave like Christian adults. They responded appropriately. It kept me out of the middle of the dog fight. It also resolved the problem and built a stronger ministry team.

One of the occupational hazards of caring for others is believing we can *fix* people. *News flash: we cannot!* It is the role of the Holy Spirit to heal, lead, and make people whole. Our job is to support the working of the Spirit in people's lives through prayer, encouragement, discernment, and when the time is right, action.

When one first gets involved with life-changing ministry, it is *intoxicating.* I chose this word intentionally. You become like a drunk who jumps into every fight. It is such an adrenaline rush to help people. Somehow, it stops being about them and becomes about you. You find yourself telling "war stories" to other Christians about tough situations you were able to handle with skill and determination. Of course, you tend to spiritualize it with religious phrases like *"I just praise God for..."* but it remains ugly. It is easy to get drawn into these unhealthy interactions. I know, I've been there. This can become a toxic threat to your ministry. Notice the similarity in the words *intoxicating* and *toxic.* Don't let your passion for ministry become obsession. It can blind you to your own need to be needed. It is a sickness that is actually makes people worse.

We already have one Messiah; that is enough. You are not Him. We serve a jealous God who will not honor any competitors. Give to others in a way that protects your spiritual and physical life and the health of your family and ministry.

"Yet for us there is but one God, the Father, from whom all things came and for whom we live; and there is but one Lord, Jesus Christ, through whom all things came and through whom we live." (1 Corinthians 8:6)

Sure, you'll get hurt once in a while, even if you are very careful. Ministry involves sacrifice and risk. What you learn is that, ultimately, being careful helps the person get better. They don't want to hurt you. They don't want the guilt of having lashed out at someone trying to help. Sometimes, people just need some time. Let them know you care but be careful.

You may get bitten.

And it hurts.

In more ways than one.

◆   ◆   ◆

Where is he now? Alan Ayers lives in Lancaster, PA with his wife, Jeanne. He is an illustrator of book covers (over 800 to his credit) and has done the artwork for two children's books about *"Maxi, the Taxi Dog."* He graduated from Temple University in Philadelphia with a BFA and has received many awards for his work including Awards received include best cover art for romances in the historical category by the Published Authors Network of Romance Writers of America, and a Certificate of Merit from the Society of Illustrators, New York City, in 1989. He enjoys reading and raising Whippets and still takes to the skies for the thrill of hang-gliding (and I still envy his courage). He and Jeanne have traveled extensively to other countries as well. His favorite slogan is, tongue in cheek, *"Don't judge a book by its cover."*

Love sharpens sensitivity. The more deeply we love, the more deeply we can be hurt and the more deeply we feel joy and satisfaction.
                                                            Charles W. Conn

o o o o o o o o o o o o o o o o o o o o o o o o o o o o o o o o o

"Ponder the path of your feet; then all your ways will be sure. Do not swerve to the right or to the left; turn your foot away from evil."

—*Proverbs 4:26-27 ESV*

8

Consider the source.

Alan shared another bit of advice that has carried me far, *"Consider the source."* When evaluating the reaction or input of another, always consider from whom you are receiving this information. It makes a world of difference. *Consider the source.*

Does the person giving you feedback *love* you? Do they have your best interests in mind? My younger sister and I separate in age by sixteen months. For most of our childhood, people thought we were twins. One of my favorite pictures of us together was while traveling with our family. We were about five and six years old. There was a tall, gray water fountain at a gas station that neither of us could conquer alone. We took turns getting on our hands and knees and stood on each other's backs to get a drink of water. This inspirational and symbolic moment was captured on film. It is a snapshot of trust and cooperation. When someone has been willing to let you stand on their back for a drink of water, you are willing to trust their input. Having the attitude of a servant is part of earning the right to be heard.

Jesus said, *"No good tree bears bad fruit, nor does a bad tree bear good fruit. Each tree is recognized by its own fruit. People do not pick figs from thorn bushes, or grapes from briers. The good man brings good things out of the good stored up in his heart, and the evil man brings evil things out of the evil stored up in his heart. For out of the overflow of his heart his mouth speaks." (Luke 6:43-45)*

There are some cultures that are more astute to contextual input than others. They are called *high context* cultures. I learned this concept from an educator named Milton Creagh. Members of these cultural groups pay attention to what is being said AND the context in which it is being said. In other words, they listen to the message, IF they accept the credibility of the messenger. In relational ministry, we call this *earning the right* to share the gospel.

There are times in my life when I was actually encouraged by those who rejected and criticized me. I do not want, nor do I seek, the approval of dishonest or unethical people. They have no real power over me unless I give it to them. I want to be "blessed" by receiving the barbs of their disapproval. When you seek the approval of another, you are giving them control over you. We all want to be liked but this can be a dangerous power in the hands of people who may mean harm to us.

My ultimate allegiance is to Jesus Christ only. I mean that. All the jobs I have performed over my adult life have not been for the boss, or pay, or the accolades. My service is for Jesus Christ. I work for him. He is my boss. I fulfill the commitments of any job but ultimately, I have One boss, and he calls me to excellence. He is the source. Sometimes the crowd will love you; sometimes they will hate you. Get used to it. Your eyes must be fixed on the One walking in front of you. You are called to follow Jesus down this narrow way regardless of the response from the spectators.

Never be too *enamored* with their *cheers*.

Never be too *intimidated* by their *jeers*.

Palm Sunday *(Hosanna! Son of David!)* and Good Friday *(Crucify Him!)* are only *five* days apart. Jesus modeled a deep connection with the true Source of life that kept him centered throughout the passion. He was aware that the source of the praise and the source of the cruelty were essentially the same. He was not to be fooled.

Both crowds wanted to use him for their own purposes. And those purposes were evil; they wanted to control the Son of God in an effort to gain worldly control. The first was an effort to thwart Roman control; the second was an effort to avoid Roman retribution. Jesus had considered the source: their motives and hidden agendas.

If a friend comes to you and says, *"I'm concerned about something in your life."* Welcome him as a brother or sister who loves you. If he or she comes again and again and again, make sure the motive is pure. Are they just being critical or is this a sincere effort to help? If this is a sincere effort to help, let them know whether it really helps or not. Be grateful. If not, and their motives are not pure, be careful and be unavailable. This type of person becomes a huge energy drain.

Without a doubt, the most important way to discern all this is the Bible. This is the source by which all other sources are to be judged. The Bible is the word of God (2 Timothy 3:16-17). Jesus is the visible expression of the invisible God (Colossians 1:15).

All other sources should be evaluated in light of these factors.

Jesus did not seek the approval of others. *"If the world hates you, keep in mind that it hated me first. If you belonged to the world, it would love you as its own. As it is, you do not belong to the world, but I have chosen you out of the world. That is why the world hates you. Remember the words I spoke to you: 'No servant is greater than his master.' If they persecuted me, they will persecute you also. If they obeyed my teaching, they will obey yours also."* (John 15:18-20)

Why do we need the approval of others? Sometimes, we even seek sanction from those who mean us harm. Isn't that odd? It distracts us from seeking the approval of the only One that matters. James, brother of Jesus, reiterates this concept. *"Out of the same mouth come praise and cursing. My brothers, this should not be. Can both fresh water and salt water flow from the same spring? My brothers, can a fig tree bear olives, or a grapevine bear figs? Neither can a salt spring produce fresh water."* (James 3:10-12)

If the person giving you feedback is a "fresh water" person, then pay attention to their input! It is difficult to confront someone and their willingness is an example of incredible love. This is called accountability. They may be trying to save your sorry self.

Don't take everything to heart. *Consider the source.* Is it a fresh water spring person or not? If he or she is trying to manipulate or control you, then you may be experiencing the transition of an old friend into a new acquaintance.

Be wise. *Consider the source.*

*The real measure of your love is what you are willing to do
for those from whom you can expect nothing in return.*
Charles W. Conn

o o o o o o o o o o o o o o o o o o o o o o o o o o o o o

"Drink water from your own cistern, running water from your own well. Should your springs overflow in the streets, your streams of water in the public squares? Let them be yours alone, never to be shared with strangers. May your fountain be blessed, and may you rejoice in the wife of your youth.

—Proverbs 5:15-18 NIV

9

Your first ministry is to your family.

Joyce Hayes is an amazing woman. She was my first real boss in my first full-time position at the Christian Education Center in Gainesville, Georgia. She is a social worker with two master's degrees, one from seminary. Joyce is a classic Southern Belle with all the warmth of the antebellum south and the strength of a Zulu warrior. Never underestimate the gentleness, strength and determination of a Southern lady!

Joyce is full of surprises as well. She loves adventure and is as likely to be crawling around in the Amazon River basin or visiting Vietnam or white-water rafting down the Nantahala River in North Carolina as she is to be teaching in a classroom or leading a workshop.

When I interviewed for the position as assistant director and teacher at the Center, one of the people on the committee asked me some hard questions.

"Are you willing to work a full work week, spend two nights a week at the center counseling people, and one Sunday a month speaking at a church, telling about the work of the Center? Are you willing to give your "all" to this ministry?"

I'm sure my expression was a frown. "No." I stammered. "Maybe I am the wrong person here." The interview went on and we covered a number of other subjects. When Kathy and I returned home, I was convinced that I was not going to Gainesville, Georgia to work. I did not feel good at all about the interview.

Shortly after we arrived, the phone rang. It was Joyce.

"Hi, Bob. How are you? Did you have a nice trip back home? How is Kathy?" Small talk; it's a southern thing.

Then she got to the point. *"We were wondering how you felt about the position. Are you still considering it?"*

"Well, actually, I was concerned about the question regarding the hours required. Something just seems wrong about that for me. That just doesn't work." I thought I was closing this door.

She swung it back open.

"Oh," her sweetness and strength mingled together and flowed through the phone, *"That opinion does not fit the philosophy of our center. We liked what we heard from you. Your first ministry is to your family."*

Bingo.

I worked for over six years at the Christian Education Center. Joyce was my director for three of those years. She was a consistent leader and fun person to work with. She was a mentor who encouraged me along the way.

Joyce didn't only say these words, she lived them.

She has four children by birth and two adopted from Korea. She worked a second job in adoption placement. Her oldest daughter (who was a student in one of my first classes) also became an adoption social worker. It was through them that we learned of a darling young deaf girl in an orphanage in Ecuador, who would later become our daughter. Joyce made it all possible.

Even before this, when we adopted our first three children (a sibling group), Joyce was there to guide and encourage us. She had been through the things we were now going through. I loved her laugh as she described some of the challenges they survived as a family. There is never a dull moment in a large family. Watching her and hearing her stories gave me hope.

Your first ministry is to your family. The family was the first institution created by God and is to remain at the top of the list. This means you may have to say *"no"* to some other institutions, including the church, to say *"yes"* to your family.

Even our own adult children need to fill up emotionally from spending time with their mother and me. I am the same way with my aging parents. It's just the way God has made us. Do not neglect this vital aspect of emotional and spiritual health. Even if your parents have passed away, find the comforting memories that remind you how proud they were of you and how much they loved you.

For many people, their family of origin is not available to them. For whatever reasons, they have become estranged. This is one of the places where the intergenerational role of the church is so important.

Some have left families when they accepted Christ. The church becomes a surrogate family to embrace these individuals. We find new role models of father, mother, brother, sister and extended family.

But let me hasten to say, every person, and I mean every person, regardless of their situation must come to peace with their family of origin. Forgiveness and redemption are the hallmarks of the Christian faith. This does not necessarily mean you approve of their choices; you must be able to forgive them for their failures to be able to move on emotionally. Do not let Christian leaders and role models become permanent substitutes for the family God put you in. These positive influences serve to show you a better way but you must come to personal peace with your birth or adoptive family. *Family is a place where you learn to love people who you sometimes don't like.*

Please don't use family as an excuse for poor quality work or lack of dependability. It is an insult to others to kick up dust about *"family first"* as a way around reasonable responsibilities. It implies that others don't share this same priority and if they did, they would also be unable to be productive. This is especially offensive if the rest of your life seems to have plenty of time for recreation and leisure. Give your best. Keep your priorities in order. God will bless this commitment to be a caring person who realizes what your first ministry is.

If you live with a high level of personal integrity, you will find as Joyce Hayes modeled for me, there is still plenty of time in your schedule for consistent caring for other people. When you make your family a priority in your life, your light shines more brightly to a world that is largely unfamiliar with healthy families.

I almost understood this before meeting Joyce.

But she showed me how it works, and I am grateful.

Your first ministry is to your family.

"For this reason I kneel before the Father, from whom his whole family in heaven and on earth derives its name. I pray that out of his glorious riches he may strengthen you with power through his Spirit in your inner being, so that Christ may dwell in your hearts through faith. And I pray that you, being rooted and established in love, may have power, together with all the saints, to grasp how wide and long and high and deep is the love of Christ, and to know this love that surpasses knowledge—that you may be filled to the measure of all the fullness of God." (Ephesians 3:14-19)

◆   ◆   ◆

Where is she now? Joyce Hayes lives in Gainesville, Georgia with her husband, Nath. They have six children, Lisa, Natalie, Tom, Heather, Tim, and Kim. She is the Director of International Adoptions for Bethany Christian Services in Georgia. In the right mood, she likes to do yard work and gardening. She is a world traveler. In her own words, *"I can honestly say (please don't think I am being pious or hyper-religious) that God is my best friend and that without this friendship, I could never have gone through some of life's hardest moments."* Her favorite sayings are *"You gain strength, courage and confidence by every experience in which you stop and look fear in the face…You must do the things you think you cannot do…."* Eleanor Roosevelt. Other favorites are… *"we are continuously faced with great opportunities brilliantly disguised as problems…don't give up and don't give in…. give more than you planned to give…open your eyes and see things as they really are…for a* *single woman, preparing for company means wiping lipstick off the milk carton...and, life is too short to dance with ugly men."*

Whosoever neglects his child to serve the Lord misunderstands the Lord, cheats his child and deceives himself.
Charles W. Conn

o o o o o o o o o o o o o o o o o o o o o o o o o o o o o o

"Deliver yourself like a gazelle from the hand of the hunter, And like a bird from the hand of the fowler."

—*Proverbs 6:5 NKJV*

10

First they appreciate it, then they expect it, then they're mad when you don't deliver.

Rufus Larkin is the most brilliant of all my mentors when it comes to human relationships. His knowledge base is immense. He has the equivalent of two doctorates, one in Clinical Psychology and the other in Social Work Counseling where he completed his doctoral dissertation. But I believe this is not where Rufus learned most of his insights. His father and mother, and his interactions with his many brothers and sisters were primary sources.

Rufus also learned many of these lessons from being an African-American male in a white-dominated society. Generally, I find people from various ethnic groups in our society to be more insightful than the majority population when it comes to the dynamics of social interactions. When you are part of a minority group, you tend to pay attention to personal interactions; particularly with those in the majority populous. If you don't, you may be compromised, co-opted, or killed. Parents in these ethnic groups tend to teach their children at a very early age to take careful notice of their surroundings, to pay attention to what is *really* happening.

One of the many things Rufus taught me was to be careful about rushing in to help people. Such efforts may actually make people weaker. Ironically, in the long run, it may also create a negative response to your efforts at kindness. Rufus used the phrase, *"First, they appreciate it. Then, they expect it. Then they're mad when you don't deliver."*

Wow. Think back over your experiences. You will certainly be able to recount numerous times that you experienced this pattern.

The phone rings in your office. It is someone needing a ride to a doctor's appointment. You think, *"This will be an opportunity to do something nice for them."*

"Sure! I'll be glad to pick you up."

They are grateful. *"THANKS!"*

When the next month comes around, your phone rings again. They are hoping you will drive them again. You are a bit surprised. Your response is a little hesitant but you agree to help again. "You set up another appointment for next week? You need me to drive you where? Okay, I guess so."

This time, the recipient of your kindness is bit less grateful and more demanding. They expected you to help. *"Okay, be sure to pick my up on time. I hate being late."*

One month later…you are surprised to learn they are depending on you for a ride to the doctor. It is a total interruption to your day. Besides, you assumed you made it clear that you were glad to help that one time. You try to be firm. "What? No, I'm sorry. I have a conflict. I cannot take you to the doctor's appointment."

They are upset. They may even throw in a barb about your faith and the old *Oh, I thought you were a Christian* assault. They could have made other arrangements but thought they could depend on you. *"FINE!"* they fume, *"I GUESS I'LL JUST HAVE TO RESCHEDULE!"* Somehow, it has become *your* problem; *you're* the one feeling guilty.

Whoa, back the truck up!

"First, they appreciate it. Then, they expect it. And then they're mad when you don't deliver."

You thought you were helping…and you were. As a result, they now expect you to provide this taxi service. After all, you are a Christian.

Christians like to help people; they like being helped. Seems like a natural symbiotic relationship to them. And then, they blame you when you don't meet expectations. They become disappointed and even angry. You have now become part of their general disillusion about the goodness of life and authenticity of anyone's personal faith.

How in the world did it go from trying to *help* to being held in *contempt* in three easy steps?

Okay, start over.

What is another way to respond to this initial request?

"Did you check out the bus schedule? Do you have a neighbor who can help? How about calling the bus company and seeing if they have a special transportation system for people who have trouble riding the regular bus. *Notice: you did not volunteer to make the call. They should make their own call.* Maybe you need to find out when your sister is available to drive you and then make the appointment to fit her schedule? I'm sure you'll find something to work out. If not, let me know and we'll toss around some other ideas."

I have often wondered why Jesus hesitated to turn the water into wine at the wedding in Cana. The interaction with his mother is particularly interesting.

"Jesus' mother was there, and Jesus and his disciples had also been invited to the wedding. When the wine was gone, Jesus' mother said to him, "They have no more wine. Dear woman, why do you involve me?" Jesus replied, "My time has not yet come." His mother said to the servants, "Do whatever he tells you." (John 2:1-5)

Mary seems to recognize that Jesus will help, IF it is best for the situation. She does not even specifically ask anything of him, she simply brings the problem to his attention. When he responds with a reference to his role as the Messiah, she turns to the servants and says in effect, *"It is his decision whether to help or not."*

Jesus chose to help. He was not forced to do so. He knew this action would have consequences. He was very intentional and Mary trusted him. My guess is she had seen him say no before and knew he would act, only if it *really* helped the situation. Be helpful. Be supportive. But the key is, never do something for someone that they can legitimately do for themselves. If you do, they become weaker and more dependent. You are not helping. You are setting both of you up for frustration and disappointment.

Being an effective minister involves some level of effective discernment. As Jesus told us, *"I am sending you out like sheep among wolves. Therefore be as shrewd as snakes and as innocent as doves."* (Matthew 10:16)

Remember, the goal is to help. Help only in ways that makes other people stronger. Avoid being set-up for failure and frustration and becoming the brunt of their anger. Sometimes, this means jumping in and helping. Other situations may require supporting them in finding a reasonable solution. Occasionally, you simply let them become more resourceful by not allowing them to be dependent on you. This may mean saying *"no"* when you could actually say *"yes."*

◆   ◆   ◆

Where is he now? Rufus Larkin lives in Flowery Branch, Georgia with his wife, LaCrisia. They have two children, Krishnan and Kahlil. Rufus is an Associate Professor in the Social Work school at the University of Georgia. His areas of interest include clinical social work practice with children, adolescents, and families, outcome research, and issues in cultural diversity. He is a member of the Editorial Board for Research on Social Work Practice. Rufus has his doctorate in Social Work from the University of Georgia and his bachelors in psychology from Fort Valley State University. His research interests are in African-American issues in mainstream education, group work practice in schools, and evaluation of clinical social work interventions. Dr. Larkin has been published in a number of scholarly journals regarding the practice of social work.

When we constantly do for others what they should do for themselves, we do not help them, we cripple them.
Charles W. Conn

He who tries to repair a burning house merely provides more fuel to the fire. First extinguish the flames and then repair the building.
Charles W. Conn

o o o o o o o o o o o o o o o o o o o o o o o o o o o o o o o o o

"There are six things which the LORD hates—yes, seven things are an abomination to Him: haughty eyes, a lying tongue, hands that shed innocent blood, a heart that devises wicked plans, feet that run rapidly to evil, a false witness who utters lies, and one who spreads strife among brothers."

—Proverbs 6:16-19 NASB

11

Watch out for blind triangles.

Rufus helped me understand another simple and profound concept. Now, I know he didn't invent this. It was from the benefit of his educational background. I am grateful for how this knowledge has helped my ministry over the years.

"Watch out for blind triangles."

Real simple. One, two, three. Blind triangles can sap your energy and destroy your reputation. They are easy to be drawn into and fairly easy to avoid.

Name any three people or groups who interact.

Let's say, a teenager, a parent and a youth minister…

A student, a teacher and a parent…

Two teenagers and a volunteer youth leader…

Two neighbors and a teenage child of one…

Your spouse, your boss and you…

Your children, your spouse and you…

Your mechanic, your spouse and the insurance company…

This list is virtually endless.

There is generally not a problem with these interactions unless the triangle is blind…meaning, the communications between any two points of the triangle are not visible to but directly involve the third person.

I think Jesus referred to this as *gossip*.

Even if it doesn't involve what may be considered gossip about the other person, it is fraught with potential problems.

"He said, she said…"

"Go tell them…"

"Why would they say this...?"

No, no, no!

This is a formula for disaster! People will get hurt, confused, and misled. At best, it befuddles the issues. At worst, it destroys relationships.

Follow the recipe provided in the Bible in Matthew 8:15-17. When you have problems with someone, go directly to them. If they refuse to listen, take a trusted friend. If they still refuse to listen, bring it before the group. If they still refuse to listen, back away.

Some people use blind triangles intentionally to cause problems. Rufus would comment on people visible in the media, referred to as "leaders" in their communities, who stir things up, just so they can be the ones credited with later calming them down. It is like a firefighter starting a fire to gain notoriety and earn extra pay. The fire is just as hot whether accidental or intentional; people get hurt.

Other people use blind triangles to hide. They hate confrontation. So they set someone else up to make the call, explain the problem, or fix the situation. Don't let them hide. Teach them the importance of basic problem solving skills. Encourage them to trust people enough to be honest and direct.

Others live from crisis to crisis. They control the flow of information as a way to manipulate others. They do not particularly want to be well. They prefer relationships that are sick. The psychological reasons are complex but the outcome is perpetual discord. Blind triangles are the drug of choice for those addicted to crisis.

You may feel a strengthening of the relationship with one person of the triangle by focusing your energy on the third person. It creates a common purpose between two points of the triangle potentially developing a false sense of rightness, *"How are WE going to help this person?"* It becomes a drama of passion and intensity. This is hurtful and can be harmful.

A final group of people sincerely believes they are helping so they dig themselves waist deep in the muck of other people's problems; the messier, the better. Focusing on the problems of others is a way for these people to ignore their own problems. Unfortunately, the sewage is no cleaner for having waded in...and the *"helper"* is a LOT dirtier.

Blind triangles have split churches and broken up families. They have brought down empires. Julius Caesar and his trusted advisor, Brutus are an example of the consequences of broken relationships, deceit and blind triangles.

What is our response?

Take the *blindness* out of the triangle or take the *triangle* out of the blindness.

Deal with people directly. Interact with two or more people openly and honestly. Never change your comments simply to suit your audience.

The relationship between Jesus and his cousin, John the Baptist is our model. There was a blind triangle between them and the people. John was stuck in prison so he sent two of his followers to ask Jesus about his ministry.

"John the Baptist sent us to you to ask, 'Are you the one who was to come, or should we expect someone else?' At that very time Jesus cured many who had diseases, sicknesses and evil spirits, and gave sight to many who were blind. So he replied to the messengers, "Go back and report to John what you have seen and heard: The blind receive sight, the lame walk, those who have leprosy are cured, the deaf hear, the dead are raised, and the good news is preached to the poor." (Luke 7:20-22)

Jesus and John took the blindness out of the triangle. Jesus instructs the two messengers from John to give direct testimony as what they observed. *"Go ask the people"* he implies. *"Do not operate on rumor and innuendo. See for yourself."*

Jesus took the triangle out of the blindness by collapsing the triangle into a straight line between only two people. His relationship was with John, his cousin. Jesus would not let the relationship go through a third party, John's disciples. John knew who Jesus was. John proclaimed, *"Look, the lamb of God, who takes away the sin of the world!"* Jesus went straight back to the already established relationship.

I have a physical reaction I call the *"Whoa. Drop Back!"* posture when I recognize a blind triangle. I hold my hands up like I am being held up, draw a short breath and take a half step back. It is the position of one about to dart out the door. I rarely run but this physical movement helps remind me of the inherent dangers in blind triangles.

Life is way too short to waste time locked in blind triangles. They are a pit for draining energy. Go directly to the source of a problem and be careful what you say, especially about another point on the triangle. Be focused on solving the problem at hand, not assigning blame.

Make your *"yes"* a simple *yes* and your *"no"* a simple *no*. (Matthew 5:37) Stay out of blind triangles.

We never know how great a matter shall become once it is begun.
The size of a fire is not determined by the spark that sets it.
Charles W. Conn

○ ○

"Listen as wisdom calls out! Hear as understanding raises her voice! She stands on the hilltop and at the crossroads. At the entrance to the city, at the city gates, she cries aloud, "I call to you, to all of you! I am raising my voice to all people."

—*Proverbs 8:1-4 NLT*

12

Never take the junkies
into your home.

Jabo Cox was a minister unlike any I had ever met or have encountered since. He could curse like a sailor and heal like a saint. His frame was wiry. His intense eyes could burn directly into you though they were usually full of compassion. Jabo survived many battles on the urban streets of New York and in rural roads of Tennessee including his own personal ones. He returned to these mean streets with the love of Jesus Christ. He was full of love.

Jabo was a junkie; at least, that's how he would describe himself. Really, he was an ex-junkie. Jesus Christ cleared his heart and veins from those years of heroin addiction. He would tell the story of a young woman named Sunshine reaching out to him with the love of Christ. He spent the rest of his life reaching out to others, including lots of teenagers and Junkies.

"Jabo," one of the teenagers from his outreach once told him. *"You know, you're the only minister I've ever met."* Sad comment; tragic commentary.

When I met Jabo, his body was a wreck. He had suffered two strokes, cancer, had cataracts and seizures. He was poor as a church mouse. He had a wonderful, loving wife, Leona, two delightful grown children and a couple of grandkids. His children faced some difficult times including his twenty year old son's bout with cancer.

Jabo would sometimes smile and remark, *"You know, if you moved the "o" and dropped the "a" you would have Job. Old Jabo is really Old Job."* And then he would laugh. He had a wonderful, high pitched laugh.

Once someone was writing a book about him called "Just Plain Jabo." He loved that title. He would chuckle and repeat, *"Just Plain Jabo. Yep, that's me."*

Jabo's spirit was simple, but intense. He knew that Kathy and I were deeply committed to ministry. He knew we had sincere hearts. One time, he told me I could make it in ministry with inner-city teens because, *"You got a heart full of love."* What incredible and kind encouragement that was to a young minister.

But the best advice he gave was direct and unwavering. He knew in our innocence we needed to hear this profound advice.

"Never take the junkies into your home."

"What?" I responded. "Why not?"

Jabo continued solemnly. *"I did this. I remodeled the second and third stories of our home for this purpose. At one time, we had over a dozen junkies living in our home while they were trying to recover…it was a mistake. We paid a price. My family suffered as a result. Never take the junkies into your home."*

I was dumbfounded. I thought good ministers were like Protestant versions of Mother Teresa with whole colonies full of lepers. What in the world did Jabo mean?

"Keep your home separate. Never take the junkies into your home."

Wow. Keep my home separate. Keep my home a place of rest and refuge. Keep my home a home. Buy another building for the junkies in my life; but return home to my spouse and children, and place of love. Protect our children. Protect our home. Protect our privacy. I thought of the time we let a woman and her baby live with us for a few days. A month later we were desperately trying to move her out. I thought of other similar situations. We had no barrier between our home and our ministry.

Being a "junkie" is not just about drugs. Jabo used this word to describe anyone you are trying to help; anyone who has significant problems. Invite people in as guests but be able to send them out, as well.

When Jesus healed the man possessed by a legion of demons, the man wanted to join the disciples and travel with them. Jesus sent him home. *"As Jesus was getting into the boat, the man who had been demon-possessed begged to go with him. Jesus did not let him, but said, "Go home to your family and tell them how much the Lord has done for you, and how he has had mercy on you." So the man went away and began to tell in the Decapolis how much Jesus had done for him. And all the people were amazed." Mark 5:18-20.* We don't know the reasons Jesus sent the man away but we can assume the man was not ready to join Jesus' band of disciples. Jesus protected the unity of this diverse group of followers. Maybe he was protecting their safety as well.

Jesus was surrounded by multitudes, followed by many, discipled a dozen, shared deeply with a few, and had one beloved friend who was the only apostle standing by Jesus' mother during the horrors of the crucifixion. Jesus withdrew from all human contact at times to bask solely in the presence of God. He was intentional about finding balance between giving to others while protecting himself emotionally and spiritually. Jesus kept his life centered and balanced; until the fullness of time.

How do you balance this with his words in Matthew 25:35-40? *"For I was hungry and you gave me something to eat, I was thirsty and you gave me something to drink, I was a stranger and you invited me in, I needed clothes and you clothed me, I was sick and you looked after me, I was in prison and you came to visit me.' "Then the righteous will answer him, 'Lord, when did we see you hungry and feed you, or thirsty and give you something to drink? When did we see you a stranger and invite you in or needing clothes and clothe you? When did we see you sick or in prison and go to visit you?' "The King will reply, 'I tell you the truth, whatever you did for one of the least of these brothers of mine, you did for me.'"*

In this scriptural narrative, each of these acts of kindness come from a centered life; from a home that is secure, has food, beverage, and clothing to share. Notice that strangers are not *"moved in"* they are *"invited in."* Taking care of someone who is sick does not mean they become a house guest. Home is a place to return after visiting someone in prison. It is also one of the locations we invite people into, along with the church, community, and workplace. Home is the hub and source of strength for doing ministry. This is one of the reasons it is so important to protect it.

This is how you take care of your first ministry–your family. I understand that sometimes in ministry you make an exception to this rule but at least establish the standard of protecting your home. It is part of being able to sustain in ministry without burning out or getting hurt.

Remember, Jabo was a junkie (ex-junkie) and we took him in. He was sick and we looked after him. He was hungry and thirsty, and we gave him food and drink. Although Jabo was certainly no danger, this is a paradox of ministry; you are called to take risks. At the same time, you have a responsibility to protect your family by minimizing risks. Your domicile is a place of ministry that must be kept sacred and separate.

Probably one of the main reasons Kathy and I are still able to give to others, year after year, is that we listened to Jabo. We have not burned out, broken up or given up. Sure, we've had people live with us for short periods of time. Sure, we've adopted five older children who were in the social service system and needed families. Sure, they have emotional baggage and there were times when they became violent. We all survived and even thrived. We are not afraid to minister. We are not afraid to get our hands dirty. But we've always protected our home. It is a safe place.

Keep your home a safe haven; a place for family.

Pretty good advice from an old junkie.

◆   ◆   ◆

Jabo Cox is survived by his wife Leona and two children, David and Angela and his four grandchildren. Jabo graduated from *Luther Rice Bible College and Seminary* when it was located in Jacksonville, Florida (it moved to Lithonia, Georgia in 1991). He was involved in ministry in Jacksonville, Florida and the Orlando area and was in the process of establishing the *New Hope Ministry* in Eatonville, Florida, when his health declined. As an interesting note, established in 1886, Eatonville is the oldest remaining African-American town in our country. Jabo reminded me of Jesus Christ in the way he could be intimidating to the pious and so gentle to the broken-hearted. His favorite scripture is often referred to as the "Love" chapter, 1 Corinthians 13, *"If I speak in the tongues of men and of angels, but have not love, I am only a resounding gong or a clanging cymbal. If I have the gift of prophecy and can fathom all mysteries and all knowledge, and if I have a faith that can move mountains, but have not love, I am nothing. If I give all I possess to the poor and surrender my body to the flames, but have not love, I gain nothing. Love is patient, love is kind. It does not envy, it does not boast, it is not proud. It is not rude, it is not self-seeking, it is not easily angered, it keeps no record of wrongs. Love does not delight in evil but rejoices with the truth. It always protects, always trusts, always hopes, always perseveres. Love never fails. But where there are prophecies, they will cease; where there are tongues, they will be stilled; where there is knowledge, it will pass away. For we know in part and we prophesy in part, but when perfection comes, the imperfect disappears. When I was a child, I talked like a child, I thought like a child, I reasoned like a child. When I became a man, I put childish ways behind me. Now we see but a poor reflection as in a mirror; then we shall see face to face. Now I know in part; then I shall know fully, even as I am fully known. And now these three remain: faith, hope and love. But the greatest of these is love."* This scripture describes Jabo well.

Books can be bought with money; knowledge can be got by study; but wisdom comes only from experience and an understanding heart.
Charles W. Conn

o o o o o o o o o o o o o o o o o o o o o o o o o o o o o

"Good sense and sound judgment can be yours. Listen, because what I say is worthwhile and right. I always speak the truth and refuse to tell a lie. Every word I speak is honest, not one is misleading or deceptive. If you have understanding, you will see that my words are just what you need."

—Proverbs 8:5-9 CEV

13

I'll never curse my God!

Jabo was a story-teller. His father owned a gas station on a curve on *Thunder Highway* in Tennessee. It was the home of bootlegged whiskey and rural living at its worst. Jabo claimed it was the meanest place on earth.

Jabo learned to play guitar to accompany his mother, Ma-maw Music, who played steel guitar for the circus. She loved the sound of Hawaiian guitar. Ma-maw Music never liked playing *hillbilly music*, later to be known as Bluegrass. I've often wondered how different her life would have been if she had ridden the Bluegrass wave. She might have become a very famous lady in the world of country music.

Jabo went to New York City during the 1940s to make his way in the music world. Unfortunately, in the smoky bars and hotels of the city, he found more than he bargained for. He discovered marijuana, cocaine, and finally, heroin. It was part of that underground culture that almost took him underground, permanently. He had to sell his body to support this habit. Not so glamorous, is it? Through the grace of God, Jabo survived and emerged as a strong minister of the gospel.

When we knew Jabo, he was frail from over ten years of battling cancer. Kathy and I lived in a city with regional health care so Jabo would often be in town for treatment. I remember bringing various teenagers to visit Jabo while he was in the Veterans Administration hospital. I knew he was in incredible pain but he loved being around young people. He had given his life to ministry with inner-city teenagers.

Jabo would sit up in his bed and look deeply into the souls of these teens. He was magic with them. I stood there in awe as he performed spiritual surgery right before my eyes. It was like watching Jesus heal the lepers. It didn't matter that over thirty-five years separated the ages of Jabo and these teens. He loved them with a simple, pure love that completely removed any barriers they normally kept in place. It was amazing to witness.

Jabo needed a place to stay when he came to town for chemotherapy and various other doctor's appointments. Often, he would stay with us. One night, I heard this strange sound coming out of the guest bedroom. At first, I thought Jabo was laughing with one of his high-pitched, hearty belly-laughs. *No, he was sobbing.* I had never heard Jabo cry.

I crept into his room.

"Jabo?"

He was lying on his side on top of the covers. He abruptly leaned up and looked at me; his large blinking eyes accentuated by previous cataract surgery, strong magnification of his glasses and his thin, gaunt body. His cheeks were wet with tears.

"WHY?" He cried. *"What is it all worth? You spend your life serving God, helping other people, and then you suffer like this!"*

For the next hour or so, I said nothing. I was still young enough to want to give answers to his anguish. By the grace of God, I was also smart enough to keep my mouth shut…and just listened to him.

"Look around at all the worthless scum who destroy other people's lives and live to be a hundred! It's not fair!"

"My son! My son! He's only twenty years old! He's never done anything wrong; no one deserves getting cancer."

"What's it worth? Why try to be a good person? Why try to make a difference in the world? I've ministered to others most of my life; who has ministered to my children? No one!"

And on. And on. There was no whining; only an intense, honest encounter with God. His small frame was wracked with grief. Here was a man standing nose-to-nose with the Creator of the universe asking hard, painful, honest questions.

I just watched and prayed. I knew God could take it. Besides, I was clueless.

Towards the end of this experience, when his burden was almost totally given over to our Lord, he grabbed my arm and looked me in the face. He spoke with the resolve of a man standing before a firing squad for his faith.

"But I will NEVER curse my God!"

"I will never curse my God!"

"I will never curse my God!"

He let go of my arm and lay back down. My heart was racing. I knew it was time to leave him alone. I backed away and paused in the doorway before exiting the room. I had been silent for about an hour. I turned and spoke to him quietly.

"Jabo, I love you. Good night."

Most of us will never face as dark a night of the soul as Jabo but certainly all will experience personal tragedies. Be honest with God about your feelings. He can handle it; your swearing, and crying, and stomping around. But may we all be like Jabo, and Job, and others who have faced struggle before us. Remember who you are addressing but keep on expressing and never curse our God.

Jabo was not talking about profanity. He was describing a cursing much deeper than language. He was speaking of a loss of belief in the sovereignty and goodness of God. He is our Lord and worthy of praise and respect, regardless of the situation. He is also worthy of our trust that He loves us and will cradle us when we suffer.

We curse God when we stop loving Him; when we forget that He knows us best…and loves us most. He will see you through until the new day.

Job 29:11-17
"Whoever heard me spoke well of me, and those who saw me commended me, because I rescued the poor who cried for help, and the fatherless who had none to assist him. The man who was dying blessed me; I made the widow's heart sing. I put on righteousness as my clothing; justice was my robe and my turban.
I was eyes to the blind and feet to the lame.
I was a father to the needy; I took up the case of the stranger.
I broke the fangs of the wicked and snatched the victims from their teeth."

Faith is based on reason even when its reasons are not seen.
Charles W. Conn

o o o o o o o o o o o o o o o o o o o o o o o o o o o o o o o

"You'll recognize this as true—you with open minds; truth-ready minds will see it at once. Prefer my life-disciplines over chasing after money, and God-knowledge over a lucrative career. For Wisdom is better than all the trappings of wealth; nothing you could wish for holds a candle to her."

—Proverbs 8:10-11 MSG

14

People are doing just about the best they can.

Kathy Ayres deserves an entire book. As cliché as it sounds, she is my soul mate. We have enjoyed a quarter of a century of new challenges, adventures, and shared hope; we pray for many more years to enjoy this life together.

When Kathy finished college, we were deciding on how to build our family. As far as we knew, Kathy can bear children but she chose to become a mother in a different way. There are older children, in the foster care system, who need a family. We decided to build our family through adoption.

It's interesting to me that Kathy never once expressed any hesitation or second thoughts about this decision. Kathy will be the first to say that there's nothing intrinsically heroic about adopting children, even older ones. Our oldest three, Christina, David, and Casey, were adopted as a full sibling group when they were the ages of one, two, and three; they're now in their twenties. In a matter of a few days, we went from no children to three. In 1993, we adopted Ana when she was eight years old. A year later, we adopted John who was nine years old at the time.

We have five children with a four-and-a-half year age spread between the oldest child and youngest. At one time, we had five teenagers. No big deal. It was the pre-teen years that about killed us! Especially when we traveled, we used to call ourselves a "high impact" family. We still take up a lot of space in a restaurant or at a friend's house.

Besides being a wife and mom, Kathy is also a career person. She works in the school system as an Occupational Therapist with special needs children. The work she does helps children overcome disabilities that create barriers to a quality education. It is a stressful job that involves hours of meetings, paperwork and direct therapeutic interventions. Kathy is one of those people who can accomplish incredible feats with apparent ease. On top of home and career, she still finds time to volunteer with a ministry for Deaf teenagers.

Now, don't let me mislead you. She is a hard-headed woman and difficult to live with at times. Sometimes, she makes me crazy with her woman inspired moods and obsessive behavior. There is certainly a tendency on her part to believe there is really only ONE best way to accomplish a task; her way. I tease her about being like a bulldog; she can bite and breathe at the same time!

But a long time ago, when we were first dating, she said something that really stuck in my mind, and has helped our marriage and my perspective on life in general.

"People are doing just about the best they can."

I don't want to believe this. I don't want to think people are doing their best; certainly they can do better. I want to believe that most people are not doing anywhere near as well as they can. I would like to blame people for their own problems, attributing it to bad attitudes, or laziness, or bad families, or choice. It is much easier to be angry with people than to believe they are giving their best effort.

What if people *really are* giving their best effort to make it through each day? Maybe, they just don't understand that life can be better. Is this why so many daughters of alcoholics marry alcoholics? Could this be the reason so many sons of abusive fathers become abusers themselves? It is not because they like it; maybe they don't know it can be any better. Maybe they feel trapped by their own expectations.

In seminary, I heard a fictional story about a thief who stole a priceless oriental rug and sold it in a pawn shop for $99. When apprehended by the police, he was asked why he pawned it for such a low amount. The thief seemed surprised and then replied, *"Oh, you mean there's a number higher than 99?"*

I once learned about a culture that only had two numbers: *"One"* and *"More Than One."* How could you expect those from this tribe to handle complex algebraic formulas? This culture has survived and even has rudimentary commerce. They are doing the best they can. I must admit, I manage my bank account with about this same level of sophistication yet I manage to survive. *I'm doing about the best I can.*

Is Kathy right? Are people really doing about the best they can? Is this why Jesus was so patient with sinners and so critical of the self-righteous? Is this part of the reason Kathy is so full of love for others? Is this why she focuses on finding ways to help others improve? Is this the way Jesus sees us? He could have cast the first stone at the woman caught in the act of adultery; he had no sin. Instead, he responded with gentleness, *"Go now and leave your life of sin."* (John 8:11) Jesus tells us there is a huge distinction between religion and relationship; or the *law* and the *spirit of the law.*

People need accountability for growth and change. With knowledge comes accountability. Christ takes us as we are but doesn't want us to remain that way. His call is to *"Come, follow me."* This means we should become more like Jesus as we walk in his steps. This also means we begin to see people as who they can be, not just who they are now. We recognize that although they may be doing about the best they can for now, they can still change through the power of the Holy Spirit.

Paul tells us in Romans 12:1-2, *"Therefore, I urge you, brothers, in view of God's mercy, to offer your bodies as living sacrifices, holy and pleasing to God–this is your spiritual act of worship. Do not conform any longer to the pattern of this world, but be transformed by the renewing of your mind. Then you will be able to test and approve what God's will is–his good, pleasing and perfect will."*

God's *"good, pleasing and perfect will"* is for us to experience abundant life full of meaning and hope. This includes transformation *"by the renewing of your mind."* We change from the inside out. Learning this perspective from Kathy has helped me accept the imperfections of others. It makes it easier for me to deal with her flaws. It has helped her deal with mine. We are both doing just about the best we can, in any given situation.

Kathy and I try to give each other our best. It's the greatest gift one can give. We are not perfect people but there is a basic trust in the goodness of the relationship and sincerity of each other.

One of my favorite defenses, when I have made a mistake is *"Well, it seemed to be the right thing at the time."* I am being truthful. I don't make mistakes on purpose. I am doing the best I can.

Since I cannot rely on my perfection, I must rely on her grace…and she must rely on mine. In fact, this is the nature of God's grace; while we were yet sinners, Christ died for us. As difficult as it may be to accept, sometimes…*people are doing just about the best they can.*

◆   ◆   ◆

Where is she now? Kathy Ayres lives in Louisville, Kentucky with her husband Bob and their five children, Christina, David, Casey, John, and Ana. She is a graduate of the University of Florida in Occupational Therapy. She enjoys outdoor activities and has an excellent eye for editing what her husband writes. Kathy was honored with a 2002 H.E.R. Award (Honoring Excellent Role Models) with the *Wise Woman Award* from *Today's Woman* magazine. Kathy is a regular volunteer with an outreach ministry to Deaf and Hard-of-Hearing teenagers called *DTQuest* (DeafTeen Quest). She was the co-founder of DeafYouth Ministries, the parent organization of *DTQuest*. Kathy's favorite scripture that reflects her priorities is found in Isaiah 61:1-3—*"The spirit of the Lord God is upon me, because He has anointed me to bring good tidings to the afflicted; he has sent me to bind up the broken-hearted, to proclaim liberty to the captives, and the opening of the prison to those who are bound; to proclaim the year of the Lord's favor, and the day* *of vengeance of our God; to comfort all who mourn;…the planting of the Lord, that he may be glorified."*

The way of Christ is believing, the blessing of Christ is belonging, the effect of Christ is behaving, the process of Christ is becoming.
Charles W. Conn

o o o o o o o o o o o o o o o o o o o o o o o o o o o o o o o

"Wisdom has built her spacious house with seven pillars. She has prepared a great banquet, mixed the wines, and set the table. She has sent her servants to invite everyone to come. She calls out from the heights overlooking the city. "Come home with me," she urges the simple. To those without good judgment, she says, "Come, eat my food, and drink the wine I have mixed. Leave your foolish ways behind, and begin to live; learn how to be wise."

—Proverbs 9:1-6 NLT

15

If you don't have time to do it right the first time, when will you have time to go back and fix it?

Bert Ayers, my oldest brother, was my hero as I grew up. He played football; so I played football. He played guitar; so I played guitar. He joined the Navy; so I went water-skiing. Bert is almost seven years older than I yet as adults, seven years becomes a much shorter period of time than when you are a child. We've become the closest of friends.

Bert became a carpenter when he first returned from the service. At the same time, we began a music group, along with Bert's wife, Debbie and our brother Alan. Other people came and went over more than four years of performing music. For much of this time, music was part-time and Bert supported his family as a carpenter.

For about one month, I worked alongside of Bert as a "Carpenter's Helper." This is a really cool name for an unskilled laborer who holds boards and occasionally hammers wood together. I particularly liked framing–nailing together two-by-four studs to make a wall–the part I liked was the ability to beat the wood into position if you happen to nail it incorrectly. It is a task full of grace and forgiveness. Even if you get it wrong, you can still whack it into place.

By the way, this was a strong motivation for me to finish my education. I definitely didn't want to make a living with my hands. I still remember two key things Bert taught me during my four week venture into the world of being a construction worker.

Bert was not one to criticize. In fact, he rarely has a negative word to say about anyone or anything. Maybe this is part of the reason people listen carefully when he speaks. He has a gentle heart and kind soul. He is strong and unafraid of conflict. It just takes a lot to get him angry.

As a young man, I was developing a tendency to curse on the job. Of course, if you've ever been around construction workers, you know this is part of the culture. I didn't want to stand out as the wimp who never worked in this type of environment.

Bert didn't even look up from his task. He just spoke softly to me.

"Hey, these guys know we're Christians. Watch what you say."

Whew. These words are particularly powerful when spoken by a brother. I started paying attention. I became much more aware of my idle words. These guys knew who my brother and I were representing and they were watching.

"Finally, brothers, whatever is true, whatever is noble, whatever is right, whatever is pure, whatever is lovely, whatever is admirable–if anything is excellent or praiseworthy–think about such things. Whatever you have learned or received or heard from me, or seen in me–put it into practice. And the God of peace will be with you." (Philippians 4:8)

The other insight I learned from Bert while ripping boards (construction lingo for sawing them) came when I was rushing through a job. I was not taking much pride in my workmanship. I just wanted to finish it and move on. Again he spoke gently.

"If you don't have time to do it right the first time, when will you have time to go back and fix it?"

Great advice. If time is tight now, why will it be more abundant in the future? Take the time to finish the task. Do it right. It is amazing how many times in my life I have been tempted to stop at good enough, paused and reminded myself of this quote.

It is interesting to notice the number of times Jesus completes a task during his ministry. Every task the Father gave him, he completed.

One example was when the woman with the issue of blood touched him in the midst of the crowd; Jesus immediately stops the parade and asks, *"Who touched me?"*

"Someone touched me; I know that power has gone out from me." Then *the woman, seeing that she could not go unnoticed, came trembling and fell at his feet. In the presence of all the people, she told why she had touched him and how she had been instantly healed. Then he said to her, "Daughter, your faith has healed you. Go in peace."* (Luke 8:46-48)

He did not delay. He took time to do it right the first time. Jesus' life was full of interruptions that he treated as welcomed guests. He would stop, focus, and act; and then he would move on. The best leaders I know how that same trait. When you are talking to them, you feel like you have their full attention to everything you are saying.

In life, it is all too easy to cut corners. It is so difficult to find time to visit a friend in the hospital, fix a meal, or even make a phone call. It is amazing how important it can be for you to just pick up the phone and make a call. If you don't have time now, when will you later? Spend less time thinking about something and more time doing it.

One of my favorite sayings is, *"If you have to eat two frogs, never think about it too long...and always eat the biggest one first."* Tackle the difficult problems of life first. Be willing to eat some frogs. It may take you away from other activities you prefer but procrastination only makes it worse. Don't waste time worrying about it.

Quality work is not a certain formula for success. Once, Bert and I started a business making and distributing popcorn. We produced an excellent product. We worked hard. We never cheated anyone. We ran a quality company. However, when it comes to financial matters, we are much better ministers than business people. We lost a great deal of money in this venture.

I had learned from Bert the importance of pride in my work, even when I fail. Never compromise excellence. Be successful in the things that really count. Ephesians 2:10 says, *"For we are God's workmanship, created in Christ Jesus to do good works, which God prepared in advance for us to do."*

If you don't have time to do it right the first time…
when will you have time to go back and fix it?

*He who takes short-cuts should not complain of rocky roads
and thorny paths.*
Charles W. Conn

○ ○

"The fear of the LORD is the beginning of wisdom, and the knowledge of the Holy One is understanding. For by me your days will be multiplied, and years of life will be added to you. If you are wise, you are wise for your-self, and if you scoff, you will bear it alone."

—Proverbs 9:10-12 NKJV

16

I'm not on that committee.

Debbie Ayers has been involved in a number of ministries over the years including a four year stay in Albania as a missionary family with her husband, Bert (my brother) and their five children. They adapted well to the culture and language in their adopted country. As anyone knows who ever lived in another country, life can be radically different in a foreign culture.

Debbie has this uncanny ability to adapt. She and Bert have lived on a navy base in Canada, a farm in rural eastern North Carolina, a small-town in Georgia, a University town, a major metropolitan area and some place so remote in Albania that we couldn't even reach them by telephone. Regardless of the setting, the Ayers family made friends wherever they went and lived as though they were home.

Now, I wish I could say the same about myself. I thought this would be true but about the same time that Debbie and Bert moved to Albania, Kathy, our three older children (Casey, David and Christina were ten-, eleven-, and twelve-years old, respectively) and I stayed for five weeks in Ecuador in the process of adopting our daughter, Ana who was eight-years old (we had not yet adopted John). The five of us landed in the Quito airport, high in the Andes Mountains around midnight. A light fog swirled around the airport lights as we exited the airplane onto the tarmac. We herded our kids and grabbed luggage while passing through groups of fully armed soldiers standing around. Scrambling through crowds, jumping into a cab, tipping almost everyone I met, being driven through the streets at breakneck speeds over numerous bumps and potholes was, to say the least, overwhelming.

Seat belts would have helped me adjust. Following some basic rules of the road would have comforted me. But no, my blood pressure was up, my breathing labored, and my nerves were on full alert.

And this was only the first hour.

It may have been the *"same old, same old"* to the locals but to me it was much more than just a language barrier; it is a complete cultural shock.

Kathy grew weary of hearing me repeat, *"I don't think we're in Kansas anymore, Toto,"* so within a day or two, she asked me to stop. This was not the first time I had left the shelter of my cave but I was amazed how ill-prepared I was for the newness of the experience. It threw me into total disequilibrium.

In contrast, Debbie seems to take everything in stride.

So, why is my sister-in-law so much better at this than I?

There is a simple and ugly truth that I hate to face about myself. I like to be in control. It is not my nature to trust other people with decisions that affect me. I don't necessarily want to control the outcomes but I definitely want to have power over the variables leading to the outcomes.

Debbie and Bert, on the other hand, recognize what is truly in their control and for the other things not in their control may remark, *"I'm not on that committee."* The key word is *flexibility.* Be able to adapt. Be open to guidance from others; and, like Debbie, bring a positive attitude to a challenge. Trust your advisors. Let others lead.

A significant part of any new experience is acknowledging our dependence on others. A healthy part of any ministry is giving up control to others. I could not fly the airplane, check the luggage, drive the cab, give directions, determine the best routes…and so forth, I had to trust others. I had to recognize that I'm not on those committees.

There is an old saying, familiar in the south that makes a similar point about conflict, *"I don't have a dog in that fight."* A friend from Birmingham, Alabama used to say this to describe the absurdity of jumping into a fight when neither side is yours. Don't join every battle; even those which are noble causes. Sometimes, just leave it alone. Stay off some committees. Know when to relinquish control to others.

Don't try to micro-manage other people. It is insulting. There are lots of dog fights you can avoid. There will be plenty of others that clearly involve you so save your strength for the ones that really matter. Choose your battles wisely.

Every church, every group of believers has its own unique culture. If you work with teenagers, recognize the distinctiveness of their culture. At the beginning, you may experience emotional vertigo. Be patient, you will learn the mores and folkways (and hearsays). Be flexible. Adapt. Avoid your need to control.

"Though I am free and belong to no man, I make myself a slave to everyone, to win as many as possible. To the Jews I became like a Jew, to win the Jews. To those under the law I became like one under the law (though I myself am not under the law), so as to win those under the law. To those not having the law I became like one not having the law (though I am not free from God's law but am under Christ's law), so as to win those not having the law. To the weak I became weak, to win the weak. I have become all things to all men so that by all possible means I might save some. I do all this for the sake of the gospel that I may share in its blessings." (1 Corinthians 9:19-23)

Debbie is a bundle of energy and usually returns from the task before anyone else rises from their seat. She maintains an excitement about life. Debbie, Bert and three of their children (two had already grown up and moved out) escaped from Albania while the country was collapsing into chaos. People were breaking into weapons storage areas, firing machine guns and other firearms wildly into the air. While trying to leave, Debbie was struck in the back of the head by a falling bullet fired into the air by someone in this crazed environment. They rushed her to the hospital. Fortunately, the bullet glanced through her scalp but did not penetrate her skull. Bandaged and dodging traffic jams and hysterical people, they made their way back to the harbor. After a harrowing escape on Italian gunboats in the middle of the night, she and two of their children were safe…yet separated from Bert, another child and a friend. Finally, about twenty-four hours later, her whole family was back together. They eventually arrived safely back in the states.

Of course, it was a terrible experience but Debbie took it all in stride. She is quick to laugh and slow to anger. How does she do this? Part of it is an issue of self-control. Most likely, it is mostly because she has little need to control others.

She feels no need to control that which is outside her responsibility.

She leaves control in the hands of the Creator.

She's not on that committee.

◆   ◆   ◆

Where are they now? Bert and Debbie Ayers live in Homestead, Florida and have five children, Kiffin, Heather, Erin, Shaun, and Kristen. Bert is the Environmental Mitigation Project Director for wetlands habitat restoration for RMC South Florida, Inc. (dba *Florida Rock and Sand*) and Debbie is the Director of the Florida Keys office of the pro-life *First Choice Women's Centers*. They both serve as Community Resource and Youth and Music Directors at *Faith Church of the Redlands* in Homestead, Florida. They enjoy teaching, traveling, missions, playing guitar and piano, photography, and singing with the family. Between Bert and Debbie, they've done undergrad or graduate work at eight different colleges or universities. Some of that was due to *being nomads* and some to the quest for the right vocations. Bert likes to quote Pogo, *"There they go, I must hasten after them, for I am their leader."*

In addition to living in Albania for four years, they have traveled to over twenty countries on four continents as missionaries or missions volunteers. Sharing their Savior and Lord Jesus with those who have never heard remains one of their foremost passions. Debbie's favorite scripture is, *"He gives strength to the weary and increases the power of the weak. Even youths grow tired and weary, and young men stumble and fall; but those who hope in the LORD will renew their strength. They will soar on wings like eagles; they will run and not grow weary, they will walk and not be faint."* Isaiah 40:29-31 Bert's favorites are *"Come to me, all you who are weary and burdened, and I will give you rest. Take my yoke upon you and learn from me, for I am gentle and humble in heart, and you will find rest for your souls. For my yoke is easy and my burden is light."* Matthew 11:28-30 and *"Who shall separate us from the love of Christ? Shall trouble or hardship or persecution or famine or nakedness or danger or sword? As it is written: "For your sake we face death all day long; we are considered as sheep to be slaughtered. No, in all these things we are more than conquerors through him who loved us. For I am convinced that neither death nor life, neither angels nor demons, neither the present nor the future, nor any powers, neither height nor depth, nor anything else in all creation, will be able to separate us from the love of God that is in Christ Jesus our Lord."* Romans 8:35-39

Peace is not so much the absence of conflict as the ability to live with it.
Charles W. Conn

o o o o o o o o o o o o o o o o o o o o o o o o o o o o o o

"The proverbs of Solomon: A wise son makes a glad father, but a foolish son is a sorrow to his mother. Treasures gained by wickedness do not profit, but righteousness delivers from death."

—Proverbs 10:1-2 ESV

17

Your greatest strengths, when overdone, become your greatest weaknesses.

Tracy Holladay and I have been the best of friends for over a quarter of a century. We are not exactly opposites but we are wired completely differently. Tracy is stable, thoughtful, insightful, intelligent and intentional. Hey, wait a minute, I'm those things too; just in a really different way! I am creative, energetic, determined, relational and intense. He is, too, but with other expressions of these traits. I guess we're really just the same, only different.

When I first met Tracy, he rented a couple of rooms in his house to Tim Dobbins and myself. I remember thinking when I met him, *"You know, Tim and I will always be close friends. I will probably know Tracy for a short period of time and then never see him again."* Twenty-seven years later, Tracy and I live two streets away from each other. I've probably seen Tim once in the past twenty years.

There is a lesson in that.

I lean on Tracy when I want an objective perspective. This doesn't mean we always agree but I respect his insights. He seems to listen to everyone in the room before rendering an opinion. It is from Tracy that I learned a saying that has been a great help over the years.

"Your greatest strengths, when overdone, become your greatest weaknesses."

If you overdo a strength, it becomes a weakness. Think about this in your own life. What are your strong points? Have they ever become a detriment by overdoing them? Do you have strong points that become an obsession for you?

For example, do you love to read? *This is a strong point.*

But does your reading become a way to escape reality? Are you ignoring other responsibilities for your reading? Does it prevent you from completing tasks? Do you quote books to others as a subtle form of pride? Do others view you as being "book smart" only? Do you begin feeling superior to others because of the books you read?

Are you a good listener? *This is a good skill.*

Yet, have you ever listened when you should have spoken up? Does active listening become a way to manipulate others? Have you lost a sense of your own opinions because you are so sensitive to the opinions of everyone else? Do you become passive-aggressive by listening when you know others want a response? Do you control others by how you listen?

Is public speaking your shining quality? *That's great!*

Have you ever said things you regret in a public setting? Have you ever unintentionally embarrassed someone with a personal story told publicly? Are you insensitive to others who are terrified of public speaking? Have you ever talked too long? Do people tease you about having a comment about everything? Do you ever talk when you should have listened? Do you assume you are always right because you are so articulate?

Are you a forgiving person? *That's scriptural.*

But, have you ever used forgiveness as a way to avoid confrontation? Does forgiveness become a way to manipulate others (they owe you)? Have you ever forgiven someone as a way to "heap guilt on their heads"? Do you let others abuse you and take advantage of you? Are you so forgiving that you don't hold others accountable for their actions?

Are you full of love for others? *That is an admirable quality.*

Are you so gracious that you forget to remind people that sin is wrong? Does love become a way to avoid telling someone the hard facts about their choices? Do you unintentionally lead people to conclude that sin is a normal and expected part of life with little or no consequences? Do you love everyone so much that no one feels particularly special, especially your children or spouse? Do you have a hard time letting go?

Are you righteous and truthful? *God wants us to be.*

Have you ever been cruel in the name of God? Do you ever feel compelled to tell people the truth about sin when what they really need, at that moment, is a friend who will encourage them? Have you ever hurt the spreading of the message of Jesus Christ because of your obsession on some doctrinal issue? Are you way too judgmental? Do you feel compelled to win every argument?

Need I go on?

Your greatest strengths, when overdone, become your greatest weaknesses.

"Brothers, think of what you were when you were called. Not many of you were wise by human standards; not many were influential; not many were of noble birth. But God chose the foolish things of the world to shame the wise; God chose the weak things of the world to shame the strong. He chose the lowly things of this world and the despised things—and the things that are not—to nullify the things that are, so that no one may boast before him. It is because of him that you are in Christ Jesus, who has become for us wisdom from God—that is, our righteousness, holiness and redemption. Therefore, as it is written: "Let him who boasts boast in the Lord." (1 Corinthians 1:26-31)

Tracy Holladay has been one of my most dependable friends. He balances out my fire and fury with his consistent, calm demeanor. I am grateful for his influence that helps put into perspective that just because something is good, more of it is not necessarily better.

The late Dr. O. Dean Martin pointed out that burn-out generally occurs by obsessing on something you love to do. You cannot *put it down* until one day you can no longer *pick it up.* You burn-out because you overdid it. Use great caution when you are working exclusively in your areas of strength. It may become your greatest weakness.

◆   ◆   ◆

Where is he now? Tracy Holladay lives in Louisville, Kentucky with his wife, Debbie. They have three children, Luke, Paul, and Anna. Tracy has been the Executive Director of *The Cabbage Patch Settlement House* (a non-profit, Christian organization that exists to empower families and children in the inner city) since July 1984. Before this, he was the Area Director for *Young Life in Kentuckiana* while in seminary. Tracy is one of the cornerstones at his church and is chided by friends for having served on almost every committee possible. His favorite walk is on any golf course and he enjoys tinkering around the house. One of his favorite scriptures is James 1:2-8, *"When all kinds of trials and temptations crowd into your lives my brothers, don't resent them as intruders, but welcome them as friends! Realize that they come to test your faith and to produce in you the quality of endurance. But let the process go on until that endurance is fully developed, and you will find you have become men of mature character with the right sort of independence. And if, in the process, any of you does not know how to meet any particular problem he has only to ask God—who gives generously to all men without making them feel foolish or guilty—and he may be quite sure that the necessary wisdom will be given him. But he must ask in sincere faith without secret doubts as to whether he really wants God's help or not. The man who trusts God, but with inward reservations, is like a wave of the sea, carried forward by the wind one moment and driven back the next. That sort of man cannot hope to receive anything from God, and the life of a man of divided loyalty will reveal instability at every turn."*

Perverted goodness becomes great evil; love becomes lust; thrift becomes miserliness; desire becomes greed; humility becomes pride; zeal becomes fanaticism.
Charles W. Conn

o o o o o o o o o o o o o o o o o o o o o o o o o o o o o o

"If you obey the LORD, you won't go hungry; if you are wicked, God won't let you have what you want. Laziness leads to poverty; hard work makes you rich. At harvest season it's smart to work hard, but stupid to sleep. Everyone praises good people, but evil hides behind the words of the wicked. Good people are remembered long after they are gone, but the wicked are soon forgotten."

—*Proverbs 10:3-7 CEV*

18

The way it is now is not the way it will always be.

Larry Rueff is an excellent physician with exceptional diagnostic skills. This means he can assess your combinations of symptoms, eliminate unlikely possibilities and eventually make a reasonable diagnosis of your illness based on this information. He starts with about a hundred possibilities based on your described symptoms, narrows it down to under ten and then decides on the three or four most likely. The amount of information Larry has crammed into his brain is amazing. He is always learning and his mind is incredibly sharp.

Larry and I have been close friends since he was in medical school. I remember the unbelievable number of hours he spent studying for his education. I was astonished at the amount of memorization of every imaginable medically-related list, the intensity of the classroom setting, and the Herculean strength needed to stay awake during rotations of days and nights without sleep. Thank goodness I was there to take him out to the local video arcade for study breaks! Breaking up asteroids and fighting off space invaders were beneficial skills for a future doctor. Those were the good old days.

When Larry finished medical school, the residency program was equally grueling. There is nothing romantic about adversity; it is just plain difficult. Larry had a saying that gave him courage for the journey:

"The way it is now, is not the way it will always be."

Simple.

Understated.

Profound.

I wonder if Larry developed this philosophy as a result of his diagnostic skills. He experiences daily the relationship between awareness, choices, and consequences. When you are able to draw from a broad base of knowledge, you begin to recognize the inevitable change which occurs over time. Things will either become better or they will become worse. The quality of our lives is largely dependent on the choices we make.

Are things miserable for you right now? *Hang in there; things will change.*

Are things wonderful for you right now? *Enjoy it; this will change, too.*

Is life boring, uneventful? *Be cool. This will change.*

Feel out-of-control? Overwhelmed? *Chill.* Everything will eventually work out all right.

The way it is now is not the way it will always be.

The point is *perseverance.*

Don't give up.

There was a guy in one of my college classes who used to proclaim boldly, *"Perseverance in the face of adversity is what made this nation great!"* I am grateful for the laughter he inspires in my memory but part of me will always respect his statement. He is right. This is part of the American psyche. Hang in there. Don't quit. Persevere. This is the closest government in history to a true meritocracy. The way it is now is NOT the way it will always be. Life will get better. Don't quit. Keep hope alive.

Suffering produces perseverance.

Perseverance produces character.

Character produces hope.

"Therefore, since we have been justified through faith, we have peace with God through our Lord Jesus Christ, through whom we have gained access by faith into this grace in which we now stand. And we rejoice in the hope of the glory of God. Not only so, but we also rejoice in our sufferings, because we know that suffering produces perseverance; perseverance, character; and character, hope. And hope does not disappoint us, because God has poured out his love into our hearts by the Holy Spirit, whom he has given us." (Romans 5:1-5)

Think about the order that scripture has laid out here. Suffering is the spark plug for the process that leads to real and lasting hope. Having a strong character is what allows us to experience a calm assurance of God's grace. This is the difference between *wishful thinking* and *hope*. Hope is costly. It cost God his Son.

There seems to be a new generation of leaders who have suffered little. They remove themselves from all things unseemly and live relatively sheltered lives. The church has become too much of a place of refuge from the evils of the world. It is dangerous to play it safe. Get into the game. Take a few hits. Get up when you are knocked down. God always calls his people to difficult tasks that require our complete dependence on him. He is interested in helping us develop our character so we can become people full of hope.

A century ago, Elbert Hubbard wrote that when we pass away and stand before the heavenly throne, *"God will not look your over for medals, degrees or diplomas, but for scars."* Maybe he wants to be sure they are not still wounds. If so, he will clean and heal them. Maybe he wants to make sure we have enough evidence of the battles we've fought for him. Maybe he will use them as a roadmap for discussing with us how he used each incident to build character in our lives, and give us hope.

If we allow it, suffering produces character. We may choose to be bitter but God can use it to make us better. Larry has now been in practice for a number of years and his work is still difficult, but he enjoys a much improved lifestyle. He has faced his share of adversity; he has persevered through times that felt impossible. But he doesn't give up when life is the most difficult. In the process, he has helped improve the lives of literally thousands of people.

The way it is now is not the way it will always be.

No, it's not easy.

Don't give up. The destination is well worth the journey.

◆   ◆   ◆

Where is he now? Larry Rueff lives in Crestwood, Kentucky with his wife Sue and their five children, Chelsea, Alex, Michelle, Heather, and Melissa. He is a physician in Internal Medicine and graduated from the University of Louisville School of Medicine. His hobbies include backpacking and gardening. He was a volunteer leader for the *Young Life* ministry for three years and on student staff for two more. His favorite scripture is Romans 10:9-10, *"That if you confess with your mouth, "Jesus is Lord," and believe in your heart that God raised him from the dead, you will be saved. For it is with your heart that you believe and are justified, and it is with your mouth that you confess and are saved."* One of the important bits of advice he often tells patients, *"People who don't give up may some day be able to reach the goal they are trying to achieve but those who quit trying, never will."*

Happiness consists in large part of knowing when to be content with things as they are and when to contend for things as they should be.
Charles W. Conn

o o o o o o o o o o o o o o o o o o o o o o o o o o o o o o

"When pride comes, then comes disgrace, but with humility comes wisdom."

—*Proverbs 11:2 NIV*

19

I just toss out the words. It's your responsibility to put them together.

Sue Rueff is as good a friend as any I've had in my life. When we first met, she was on staff with Young Life in Louisville and the team leader for our outreach to a local high school. In some of my more immature moments, I used to discretely yawn at her while she was giving club talks…to make her yawn. Even now, when she reads this she will probably yawn. How about you?

Can you feel it coming on?

Yawn.

Wow. The power of words.

Sue is fun and intelligent and filled with insight. Like all of us, she occasionally gets her sentences mixed up. She has all the words; they just may not be in the right order. It makes for some funny moments. She laughs and exclaims, *"I just toss out the words. It's your responsibility to put them together!"*

Sue is absolutely right! The people who influence us toss out their words into our lives but it is our responsibility to make sense out of them. When it comes down to it, communication is much more about depth than distance; quality, not quantity. Learning is ultimately the responsibility of the learner.

Oftentimes as caring people we feel the burden of *getting it right.* We become overly concerned with every word we utter, every conversation, how we dress, what movies we see, how others see us, yada,

yada, yada. Somehow, our focus shifts from the grace of Jesus Christ to a quasi-works method of salvation.

"I will show you what he is like who comes to me and hears my words and puts them into practice. He is like a man building a house, who dug down deep and laid the foundation on rock. When a flood came, the torrent struck that house but could not shake it, because it was well built. But the one who hears my words and does not put them into practice is like a man who built a house on the ground without a foundation. The moment the torrent struck that house, it collapsed and its destruction was complete." (Luke 6:47-49)

There are two steps in this scripture: *"hears my words"* and *"puts them into practice."* Jesus has given us the right words; it is our responsibility to put them together in a way that makes sense.

Jesus tossed out a lot of words. One collection of his sayings is found in the "Sermon on the Mount." He begins by turning the world upside down. *"Looking at his disciples, he said: Blessed are you who are poor, for yours is the kingdom of God. Blessed are you who hunger now, for you will be satisfied. Blessed are you who weep now, for you will laugh. Blessed are you when men hate you, when they exclude you and insult you and reject your name as evil, because of the Son of Man."* (Luke 6:20-22)

The world will throw lots of bad things your way. Turn them into blessings. You have the choice of how you will respond. Choose to enjoy the process. The gospel is serious business but don't take yourself too seriously.

I have two friends who are roughly the same age. One complains about virtually everything. The other almost never complains. The second friend (who is so positive) clearly has the more difficult life of the two. What is the difference? *Attitude.* My positive friend is able to take life in stride and make the best of every situation. He is also infinitely happier than my complaining friend who I think insults God with his negativity.

Casey, our middle daughter, is notoriously optimistic. One time, when she was young, a tornado brushed past our house toppling four trees in our yard. There were twisted and broken branches all over our house and property. No sooner had the sound of crashing trees and rushing wind come to a halt when Casey exclaimed, *"Oh Dad! Think of all the firewood we'll have now!"*

Life will toss out lots of things at us. How we respond tells a great deal about our character. Do you know how to laugh? Do you let yourself be optimistic? Do you seek out the best in people? Do you take time to enjoy? Do you take life seriously but not take yourself too seriously as you take life? Sometimes, just enjoy the craziness of it all.

Jesus took time to enjoy. He was constantly taking walks in the desert and sometimes on water. He seemed to love a good party. His first miracle was at a wedding celebration. He feasted in the home of Matthew and Zacheous, two well-known partiers. He hung out in the home of his good friends, Mary, Martha and Lazarus. I feel fairly confident the Jesus would have loved a good cup of Starbucks coffee. I know he enjoyed the conversation of good friends spending time together.

I believe he was fun to be around. He still is.

Laugh with the Galilean who created laughter. When he was with his Father in the beginning, did he ever break out into a big grin as he watched the forming expanse of the galaxy? Was there any giggling going on when animal after animal was brought into existence? Can you imagine his delight when he first saw man created from the dust and woman from his rib? I wonder what the word for *"Cool!"* is in Hebrew. Our God is the source and creator of *GREAT* joy!

God has given you life. It is your choice whether to dance or pout. Shall you sing or cry? Will you shake with laughter or shudder with fear? Tell God thanks for the opportunity to draw your next breath. It is a gift. Quit complaining. When the next storm comes by, focus on all the firewood you'll be able to gather.

The words of Jesus are life changing, if we let them wash over us. Put his words together in a way that brings glory to him.

And by the way, enjoy the ride.

Life tosses out the words.

It is our responsibility how we put it all together.

◆   ◆   ◆

Where is she now? Sue Rueff lives in Crestwood, Kentucky with her husband Larry and their five children, Chelsea, Alex, Michelle, Heather, and Melissa. Sue has a Masters of Science in Social Work (MSSW) from Kent School at the University of Louisville. She was on *Young Life* staff for a number of years and is currently a volunteer with a variety of ministries. She is the founding Chairperson of the Board of Trustees for DeafYouth Ministries (*DTQuest*) and on the Board for *Young Life Oldham County* where she was recently was honored with the SPIRIT award for outstanding volunteerism. She continues to be a vital part of the preschool ministry at *Northeast Christian Church*. On top of all this, she works at *Eastern Area Community Mini*stries in Louisville as the Program Director of the Older Adult Services.

Sue says that most of her hobbies include watching her children have fun…soccer, cheerleading, basketball, skate boarding, tap and ballet recitals, piano…One of her personal goals is to complete a book of recipes by her sister, Sandy, who was a gourmet chef who recently passed away, called: *"Gravy is NOT a Beverage."* As a mother of five school-aged children, according to Sue her favorite saying seems to be *"CLOSE the DOOR!!!!!"*

Fear, doubt and spiritual frigidity are thawed more quickly by the warmth of love than by the heat of argument.
Charles W. Conn

o o o o o o o o o o o o o o o o o o o o o o o o o o o o o o o

"The desires of good people lead straight to the best, but wicked ambition ends in angry frustration. The world of the generous gets larger and larger; the world of the stingy gets smaller and smaller. The one who blesses others is abundantly blessed; those who help others are helped. Curses on those who drive a hard bargain! Blessings on all who play fair and square! The one who seeks good finds delight; the student of evil becomes evil. A life devoted to things is a dead life, a stump; a God-shaped life is a flourishing tree.

—*Proverbs 11:23-28 MSG*

20

We've got to understand this thing called Christian Community.

Herb Wagemaker is a psychiatrist, researcher, author (among other things) and a passionate encourager of "Koinonia"—Christian community. Koinonia is a Greek word which is usually translated *fellowship* but has little or nothing to do with Wednesday night suppers at your average local church.

"Hi, how are you?"

"Fine, fine, fine!"

"Good to see you!"

Right. Get real.

Why is it that the place where we should find the most authenticity is where we often find the least? If the person you work with knows more about your personal life than your closest church friends, then you have a problem. If more people know your name in the local restaurant or bar or library than in church, then something is dramatically wrong. Jesus Christ has called you to experience authentic Christian community as the church. He requires it.

Koinonia is the blending together of our lives by the spirit of the living God.

Unfortunately, church can become a place where people wear masks while playing the church game—we are all smiles, all the time. The only problems we ever share are in the past tense as part of a testimony. This is not only wrong, it is dangerous. God designed us for emotional intimacy.

It was Herb who first insisted on authentic Christian community for the youth ministry volunteers under his tutelage. He influenced the people who directly influenced me. Later, Herb and I would work on the same *Young Life* team, reaching out to teenagers. I can still see Herb standing with a group of leaders, running his long, thin hand through his graying hair, leaning casually to one side. He would touch his chin and then hold his palm up for emphasis, *"Hey, guys. I think we really need to think here about the importance of building Christian community."*

At first, I would tease him about singing this same verse again and again.

Later, I found myself humming the tune, remembering the words, and finally singing this Christian community *song* with the full gusto of a drunken Irishman.

"We've GOT to understand this thing called Christian Community!"

KOINONIA! Being the body of Christ. Experiencing authentic relationships.

Christian community is so life-giving because it is the way God brings healing into the world. Kathy and I were involved with establishing a small Christian community that worshipped together called St. Luke Church. It came about largely because of painfully shallow interactions we experienced at the *big church.* We were dying for authentic relationships that weathered the test of time. Once you taste the real thing, you tend to lose interest in cheap imitations. Koinonia is where one finds wholeness.

In our evangelical traditions, we emphasize the individual. "I" was saved. Jesus redeemed "my" soul. I completely agree with the theology that calls the individual into a right relationship with the Creator through his son Jesus. But we fall short in effectively communicating that we are saved from isolation and to wholeness within a community of faith. With Jesus as the head, we become members of one body; connected and interconnected as a single organism. God draws us into deep and loving relationships with other believers for the purpose of becoming His physical body on earth.

"The body is a unit, though it is made up of many parts; and though all its parts are many, they form one body. So it is with Christ. For we were all

baptized by one Spirit into one body—whether Jews or Greeks, slave or free—and we were all given the one Spirit to drink. Now the body is not made up of one part but of many. If the foot should say, "Because I am not a hand, I do not belong to the body," it would not for that reason cease to be part of the body. And if the ear should say, "Because I am not an eye, I do not belong to the body," it would not for that reason cease to be part of the body. If the whole body were an eye, where would the sense of hearing be? If the whole body were an ear, where would the sense of smell be? But in fact God has arranged the parts in the body, every one of them, just as he wanted them to be. If they were all one part, where would the body be? As it is, there are many parts, but one body." (1 Corinthians 12:12-19)

He calls us into right relationship with our brothers and sisters in Christ. This does not mean we always agree with or even like each other. Family is where you learn to love people whom you don't like sometimes.

Community is a vital part of any Christian outreach ministry. This means we care enough to notice our relationship with other Christians as being more than empty words of affirmation and niceness. He calls us to love each other as he has loved us.

A friend once told me she puts on her *best face* so people will like her.

"That's interesting," I responded. "I try to show my worst possible self so that I know who ever still likes me is really my friend!" I'll take authenticity over popularity, any day of the week and twice on Sunday. Especially on Sunday.

Christian community is not about showing our worst possible self but about knowing you are loved, everyday...good days and bad because you are part of the body of Christ; you are family.

I'm still trying to figure this out. I appreciate Herb's influence on me and others. Herb was right, we really DO need to understand this thing called Christian community.

Jesus requires it of us.

◆   ◆   ◆

Where is he now? Herb Wagemaker lives in Ponte Vedra Beach, Florida with his wife, Marianne. They have three children, Robyn, Alex, and Lori…After completing his residency in 1972, he worked in a community mental health facility in Gainesville, Fla. In 1975, he joined the faculty of the University of Louisville Department of Psychiatry. While affiliated with the university, he directed inpatient psychiatric services at the Louisville General Hospital and continued his research in the treatment of schizophrenia. In Louisville, he also worked as a consultant to a community mental health center and was medical director of Central State Hospital. At present, Dr. Wagemaker is in private practice in Jacksonville, Fla., and continues in psychiatric research. He is the author of a number of books including *"Medications And Our Children: A Parent's Guide"," The Surprising Truth About Depression"* and *"Taming Oedipus, Boys and Violence, Why?"* Herb says their lives revolve around kids and grandkids. They also provide support for college kids through the *Young Life* ministry leadership training in Gainesville and Jacksonville, Florida. His favorite scriptures are the Kingdom Parables and the Sermon on the Mount. Teacher and author, Dale Bruner, has been a teacher for Herb; especially the impact on Herb of Dale's commentary on Matthew has been an influence on Herb.

Casual friends enjoy small talk; good friends enjoy the exchange of ideas and considerations. Rare, however, are friends who can share periods of silence, whose communion of spirit is not made frantic by a lapse in conversation.
Charles W. Conn

o o o o o o o o o o o o o o o o o o o o o o o o o o o o o o o o

"The fruit of the righteous is a tree of life, and whoever captures souls is wise. If the righteous is repaid on earth, how much more the wicked and the sinner!"

—Proverbs 11:30-31 ESV

21

Love is a commitment.

Reuben Black was a pilot for Delta Air Lines for the duration of his career. He is a self-proclaimed curmudgeon who is intimidated by no one. He is out-spoken, direct, and opinionated. He is drawn to controversy and usually takes the opposing view. There is no confusion about who loves him and who hates him. To me, Reuben is a wonderful and trusted friend.

Reuben's wife, Marjorie, is gentle and positive about everyone. She touches a place in your heart reserved for angels and children. She loves to laugh and is every bit Reuben's equal when it comes to personal strength and integrity. One of her favorite sayings, and she lives by this motto, is *"Don't sweat the small stuff…and it's ALL small stuff."* She is a delightful person.

Their marriage spans almost five decades and they have four outstanding adult children who make this world a better place. Reuben and Marj have an annual "Grandcamp" where they put all their years of experience of youth ministry into providing a week of adventure for their grandchildren. Each year brings a theme and abundance of activities. One year, a huge teepee was erected in their back yard for Grandcamp. They are incredible people.

Reuben once told me, that a number of years earlier, they experienced some trouble in their marriage. He commented that his pastor (and friend) gave him some advice that changed his thinking about relationships and *"probably saved my marriage."* I tried to mask my shock. It was difficult to imagine Reuben and Marj ever having a strained relationship. They seem to enjoy each other so completely.

Reuben continued. *"He told me, love is not a feeling; it's a commitment."*

Love is a commitment. Feelings come and go. Somehow in our society, we get the sense that commitments can be broken when feelings fade. Love is much deeper and stronger than feelings that simply come and go. Sometimes, in a relationship, you just continue to show up. If you are smart, you will continue to show up with flowers. The feelings will return but the commitment remains constant.

Look at Jesus. Did he enjoy his death? *No. He despised the cross.*

Was he willing to die for us, regardless? *Obviously. He persevered.*

"Therefore, since we are surrounded by such a great cloud of witnesses, let us throw off everything that hinders and the sin that so easily entangles, and let us run with perseverance the race marked out for us. Let us fix our eyes on Jesus, the author and perfecter of our faith, who for the joy set before him endured the cross, scorning its shame, and sat down at the right hand of the throne of God. Consider him who endured such opposition from sinful men, so that you will not grow weary and lose heart." (Hebrews 12:1-3)

Everyone deals with grief and stress differently. I am basically a private person. People may enter my pain by invitation only. When I am in tremendous grief, I shudder at the thought of being touched. It is like my nerves are on fire. Don't hug me to comfort me. Just give me space.

One time, my brother was having surgery for what may have been his last day on earth. It was an incredibly stressful time. The waiting room was crowded with his friends. I had no interest in being around these people. I had no place to sit without having to carry on small talk. The whole experience was overwhelming but most people would never have noticed. I have a knack for appearing cool under pressure.

That morning, Reuben stopped by the hospital. *What a welcomed site!* He has thick, white hair and carries himself like someone confident enough to fly huge passenger jets across the Atlantic.

He was there for me. He immediately saw through my façade and into my pain and took me downstairs for a cup of coffee. He didn't say much. We didn't join hands and sing *Kum Ba Yah.* We just sat there and chatted like two old curmudgeons.

After a while, he excused himself for a moment to make a phone call.

When he returned, I realized he wasn't leaving; he had canceled all his appointments for the day. I don't know what Delta administrators do all day but I can imagine they are busy people. He never mentioned what he gave up by being with me during my moment of need. It was a sacrifice on his part simply because of his love for me. Reuben may never know what this meant to me.

Maybe he will now.

His love for me was a commitment.

He learned this from God.

It was a long, long day but the news was excellent. They removed a benign, eight-and-a-half pound tumor from my brother's chest cavity. *Eight-and-a-half pounds! The size of a full-term baby in his chest! He could breathe again and would live!* My brother didn't even have to have follow-up chemotherapy. It was a testimony of modern science, technology, skill and the courage of the surgeon to operate on what appeared to be a hopeless case. Above all, it was a miracle.

I experienced another marvel that day, the gift of friendship. Commitment is a miracle too. Reuben showed me the magnitude of loyalty. *"Carry each other's burdens, and in this way you will fulfill the law of Christ." (Galatians 6:2)*

Following Christ is a commitment. There will be times you don't feel like a Christian. There will be moments you are embarrassed to call yourself a Christ-follower. Sometimes, God seems a million miles away and you feel utterly alone. There will be points in your life when you face overwhelming temptation. Your mind is clouded and your judgment impaired. But don't give up on what you know to be true. Love is a commitment. God loves you; this never changes.

Feelings come and go but faith, hope and love are everlasting.

And the greatest of these is love.

The kind of love that makes a commitment.

◆   ◆   ◆

Where is he now? Reuben Black lives in Gainesville, Georgia with his wife, Marjorie. They have four children, Jeff, Kathy, Patti, and Tim and many talented grandchildren. Reuben graduated from North Georgia College and is now a retired Delta pilot. During his tenure at Delta, he worked in administration for the airlines and wrote a chapter, "Cockpit Resource Management" in the *Academic Press* publication. He now makes golf and tennis balls fly and enjoys writing. He is one of the founding charter members of St. Luke Church and produces a regular newsletter called Celebrations. Reuben has been very active in Boy Scouts, mentoring, and the Elachee Nature Science Center. One of his favorite sayings, referred to as Hackman's Law is *"Be prepared. Lie in wait."*

Life's greatest happiness comes when duty and
desire are combined in the same task.
Charles W. Conn

ooooooooooooooooooooooooooooooooo
"If you love learning, you love the discipline that goes with it—how shortsighted to refuse correction! A good person basks in the delight of GOD, and he wants nothing to do with devious schemers. You can't find firm footing in a swamp, but life rooted in God stands firm."

—*Proverbs 12:1-3 MSG*

22

Those we serve are angels sent from God to teach us to fly.

Steve Brown is brilliant. He pretends to be a red-neck from the south who dips snuff, hunts and fishes but no one is really fooled. Steve is a genius with a doctorate who dips snuff, hunts and fishes. He simply treasures his roots. You learn a great deal when you grow up in the rural south. The laboratory of daily life is often a much better instructor than the most extraordinary textbook. Steve remains an excellent student of both.

Every state has at least one other state that is the brunt of its jokes. Steve was born and raised in one of my favorite targets. I loved teasing him about it. *"Steve, have you ever noticed that when you find one person from your state there seems to be a whole group of them. Why is that? Do the people who escape send money back for their friends to follow them to the Promised Land?"*

He gave a hearty laugh (although I'm not sure he appreciated my humor) and usually respond to my insult with a funny story or two. Steve was my pastor for a decade. We have now lived in different cities for another decade or so. In many ways, Steve still is my pastor. We were part of beginning a community of faith called St. Luke Church; alongside others who longed for right relationships with God, neighbors and self.

When I first met Steve, I thought he mumbled. Then I thought, *"I'm dumb as a rock. He is not mumbling; I just don't understand what in the world he is talking about."* He would say profound things that I had to stretch to understand.

Finally, I realized he was a storyteller in the tradition of the Jewish Rabbi stories. His mind was operating between multiple languages and cultures…a Yiddish, Hebrew, Greek, Southern, Rural sort of thing. He also moves through historical epochs like a time voyager. His basic three dimensional stories can easily morph into four dimensional insights. For years Kathy and I were the sign language interpreters for Steve. Wow. Now, that's a flight. But Steve was always an awesome proclaimer of the word of God.

One of Steve's sermons that stands out in my mind was how we view those whom we serve. He quietly spoke with Rabbinical wisdom, *"People we help…are angels sent to us by God. They teach us to serve. It is through them that we gain our wings and learn to fly."*

Think about these words.

People we help…*all these needy people*…are angels sent to us by God. *They are messengers.* They teach us to serve. *We are the students and they instruct us.* It is through them that we gain our wings and learn to fly. *It is how we love those whom God has sent that we draw closely to the One who created us; the One who loves us and teaches us to put our faith into action.*

We are not do-gooders; we are the beneficiaries of God's grace. Those we serve are angels sent from God to teach us to fly. We should be grateful for these messengers of God who are sent our way! They allow us to serve them and love them in the name of Jesus. Talk about respect for those whom you serve!

The Bible tells us, *"Keep on loving each other as brothers. Do not forget to entertain strangers, for by so doing some people have entertained angels without knowing it. Remember those in prison as if you were their fellow prisoners, and those who are mistreated as if you yourselves were suffering."* (Hebrews 13:1-3)

Maybe the angels we entertain are not only the celestial kind. This verse almost jumps off the page and may overshadow the verses before and after. The author of Hebrews writes of loving *each other...strangers...prisoners...those who are mistreated.* The point is particularly poignant with the last few words, *"as if you yourselves were suffering."* In other words, these are just ordinary people who need your compassion. Don't sit in judgment of their situation. Express the same love you would want for yourself. Show empathy as though they are part of your own family. Treat others as you want to be treated.

For a number of years, I was the Executive Director of a statewide non-profit organization that served people with brain injuries. As part of my job, I was interacting with people in positions of power within large corporations, the media, the legislature and those in the Governor's office. It is always interesting to note how many friends you have when you work in influential positions and how few remain after you leave.

In this position, I was never enamored by the office or those primarily motivated by money and status. I used to say publicly and privately, *"I work WITH the state, I work WITH the service providers but I work FOR the people with brain injuries."* For example, I placed my own office directly behind the receptionist's desk facing the entrance of the building and left my door open so I was completely accessible. I was much more interested in serving the people than I was in impressing those in power.

James addresses this directly in his epistle, *"Listen, my dear brothers: Has not God chosen those who are poor in the eyes of the world to be rich in faith and to inherit the kingdom he promised those who love him? But you have insulted the poor. Is it not the rich who are exploiting you? Are they not the ones who are dragging you into court? Are they not the ones who are slandering the noble name of him to whom you belong? If you really keep the royal law found in Scripture, "Love your neighbor as yourself," you are doing right. But if you show favoritism, you sin and are convicted by the law as lawbreakers."* (James 2:5-9)

It is so easy to resent those whom we serve. There is a great temptation to develop an underlying anger at people because of their misfortune; because much of it may be a result of their own choices. We sit in judgment as though we know the true hearts of others. But never forget, you are entertaining angels every day. Treat them with respect. They are teaching you how to fly into the arms of the loving Father.

When we get to heaven, it will be interesting to see who Steve Brown hangs around. I have the feeling it won't be the CEOs or Presidents or Chairman of the Boards of anything. He will likely be fishing with a motley group of angels, spitting into a cup and rearing back in laughter at a good heavenly joke or two.

Steve and the good folks at St. Luke Church have certainly learned to fly. They recognize the angels sent to them; and serve them accordingly.

◆   ◆   ◆

Where is he now? Steve Brown lives in Gainesville, Georgia with his wife, Cheryl. They have two children, Neel and Meredith. Steve has his Master of Divinity from *New Orleans Baptist Theological Seminary* and Doctorate of Ministry from *Southeastern Seminary* in Wake Forest, NC. Steve's favorite scripture is 1 John 4:7-12. *"Dear friends, let us love one another, for love comes from God. Everyone who loves has been born of God and knows God. Whoever does not love does not know God, because God is love. This is how God showed his love among us: He sent his one and only Son into the world that we might live through him. This is love: not that we loved God, but that he loved us and sent his Son as an atoning sacrifice for our sins. Dear friends, since God so loved us, we also ought to love one another. No one has ever seen God; but if we love one another, God lives in us and his love is made complete in us."* When I was getting this information Steve's comment to me, punctuated by laughter, was *"Ayres, what are you doing? Have you lost your mind by including me in a book?"*

Many a heart of gold comes wrapped in a ragged coat.
Charles W. Conn

o o o o o o o o o o o o o o o o o o o o o o o o o o o o o

"Better to be a nobody and yet have a servant than pretend to be somebody and have no food."

—*Proverbs 12:9 NIV*

23

The glass is half empty. The glass is half full. I say, 'Get a new glass!'

Marvin Highfill experienced a dramatic change in one micro-second. One morning, while working at a construction site, a worker accidentally dropped a piece of metal from fifteen stories above him, striking Marvin at the base of his skull. Seventy-two days later, he opened his eyes. Another year and a-half passed before he had working memory. He had to re-learn how to walk, talk, eat, care for himself and reenter the shaky world of independence.

Over twenty years have now passed and Marvin battles the residual effects of his brain injury on a daily basis. His center of balance changes every time he stands, his short term memory has been affected, he takes various medications for physical disabilities, he fatigues more easily than he would otherwise and has various physical problems as a result of the injury. The brain injury radically changed his life.

One moment, Marvin was working bent over in an elevator shaft and then next moment, a year-and-a-half had passed. Lying in his bed in a rehabilitation hospital and watching the news, he realizes there was a different President on the television than the one he remembered. Everything changed. His relationships were different. Few friends remained. His role in the family changed. His level of independence was greatly redefined.

But brain injury is not what defines Marvin. He is a brilliant and successful man. Marvin has been married (and widowed), is now engaged to be married, drives very nice vehicles, owns extensive property, is involved in civic and community causes, and has an amazing mind for the stock market and financial investments. His constant agenda is to improve. He recognizes his limitations and operates effectively within them. He also stretches himself to learn daily. Marvin is an insightful and loyal friend.

We share breakfast together weekly as we have for many years. In our conversations, he is usually a few steps ahead of me with broad knowledge in a range of subjects. One of my favorite sayings of Marvin's is, *"People talk about the glass being half empty, or half full. I say, 'Get a new glass!'"*

Marvin's glass got broken. The shattering of his life was tragic but not the end of the world. Over a number of years and lots of support from his family he poured himself into a new glass. He was neither half-empty nor half-full; by redefining himself based on new variables, he chose to be full again. Life is different but abundant.

Do you have a past tragedy that invades your thoughts? Are you frustrated with your physical limitations? Do you obsess on what you do not have or never will accomplish? Are you jealous of others who seem to have more than you? Does your resentment become a convenient excuse for being negative?

Accept your limitations but don't use them as excuses. Find ways to cope. Recognize your weaknesses and admit to them. Be willing to improve your life. Personal improvement begins with accepting the responsibility for change.

"What this means is that those who become Christians become new persons. They are not the same anymore, for the old life is gone. A new life has begun! All this newness of life is from God, who brought us back to himself through what Christ did. And God has given us the task of reconciling people to him. For God was in Christ, reconciling the world to himself, no longer counting people's sins against them. This is the won-

derful message he has given us to tell others. We are Christ's ambassadors, and God is using us to speak to you. We urge you, as though Christ himself were here pleading with you, "Be reconciled to God!" For God made Christ, who never sinned, to be the offering for our sin, so that we could be made right with God through Christ." (2 Corinthians 5:17-21)

You are a new person; your old life is gone. Let it go. God has brought you back into right relationship with himself. He is no longer counting your sins against you. This is a wonderful message! Now it is our job to share with others this incredible news. We can be reconciled with God. We can be made right with God through Jesus Christ.

Life is difficult at times. You may be cut by shattered glass from your past. Don't waste too much time worrying about the things you cannot change. Don't hold on to those old hurts and disappointments. Choose to enjoy this gift of life. Help others connect to this abundant life.

Marvin's other favorite saying is that his injury *"may be a reason but it's never an excuse."* There is a huge difference between a *reason* and an *excuse*. A *reason* is the reality of your life-situation and the barriers you face. An *excuse* is hiding behind our life-situation as a way to avoid personal responsibilities. Sometimes, people like to obsess on the negative things in life as a way of drawing attention; they love throwing a "pity party" and are thrilled to serve as the honored guest!

I often told my children when they were young, *"You know, feeling sorry for yourself is like wetting your pants. At first, it feels all good and warm...and then, after a while, it gets all cold and uncomfortable...and finally it just stinks."* Self-pity works at first; but eventually it only smells bad and drives people away.

I can give you a long list of things I cannot do. I cannot slam dunk a basketball, I cannot sing opera, I cannot play the piano, I cannot practice medicine or law, I cannot...I cannot...But these are not the things which define me.

On the other hand, there are a few things I do well. I've learned to accept who I am and celebrate who I am becoming. Who am I? *I am a person created in the image of God for his purposes.* He has given me these gifts. I work hard to be faithful to developing my skills. Focus on your strengths; improve on your weaknesses.

If your internal struggle for identity is due in part to a helpless feeling of being trapped by sin, I have some more advice: *"do what's right, don't do what's wrong."* Stop the behavior that causes you grief. Don't add any more painful memories to your mind. Then, fill your life with good things and good people who draw you closer to the loving God. Surround yourself with healthy people. Accept the forgiveness Christ offers. Be willing to forgive yourself. We have little control over the things in life that slam into us while we are busy at work but we each choose how we will respond.

I am an advocate of Christian counseling when life starts getting tangled. When life gets out of balance, seek help. Counselors are like any specialists; the first one you see may not have the right background and experience to help you. Be willing to find someone who is a fit. But many emotional struggles can be prevented by maintaining healthy relationships by choosing how we will live. Practice a healthy emotional lifestyle and have good, deep friendships with caring people.

These friends may even help you *get a new glass.*

◆   ◆   ◆

Where is he now? Marvin Highfill lives in Louisville, Kentucky. In 1979, Marvin was three hours away from graduating in engineering at the *Speed Scientific School* at the University of Louisville and working in the elevator trade when he sustained a brain injury in an industrial accident. He was awarded the prestigious *Bell Award* and *Jefferson Award* in 1996 for outstanding volunteerism on behalf of people with brain injuries in the Commonwealth of Kentucky. He is a member of the *Lions Club* and the *Kentucky Colonels*. Marvin's financial investments in the stock market have always been motivated by companies that improve the lives of others, not just make money. When people ask him what he wants for Christmas or a birthday gift, he usually responds, *"I just want to see a smile on everybody's face"* and he means it.

*Ultimate victory consists of getting up one time
more than we are knocked down.*
Charles W. Conn

o o o o o o o o o o o o o o o o o o o o o o o o o o o o o o o

"The teaching of the wise is a fountain of life, to turn aside from the snares of death."

—Proverbs 13:14 NASB

24

Question everything.

Ben Sharpton and I became friends while both working with teenagers over a quarter of a century ago. He, another youth minister and I met weekly to share and pray together. We built bonds of friendship that helped each of us through difficult times. Ben and I remain in regular contact to this day. I treasure his friendship. I enjoy his edginess. I chuckle at his humor. I admire his work ethic. I am impressed with his deep love for his wife and children. I appreciate his faithfulness to our friendship. I respect his liberal bent on various issues because of the integrity of his heart. Deeply committed Christians will still disagree at times. Too much agreement makes me nervous. I applaud the fact that Ben believes that faith and reason go hand in hand.

"Question everything," he told me recently. When he said it, I realized that he has lived by that creed since we first met many years ago. *"Question what you read, what you see, what you hear, your government, your teachers, your next door neighbor, the basketball coach, your pastor..."* The list goes on and on. Never fear asking life's difficult questions. Faith involves struggle. Struggle brings growth.

"Consider it pure joy, my brothers, whenever you face trials of many kinds, because you know that the testing of your faith develops perseverance. Perseverance must finish its work so that you may be mature and complete, not lacking anything." (James 1:2-4) Trials sometimes exist in the questions that plague us. Consider it a joy that we serve a God who will allow us to question what we believe. Determine *why* you believe *what* you believe. It is okay, even healthy, to ask questions of God.

Challenge your faith everyday. The goal is to become *"mature and complete, not lacking anything."*

Sometimes we experience trials like Jacob wrestling with an angel in Genesis 32:24-28. *"So Jacob was left alone, and a man wrestled with him till daybreak. When the man saw that he could not overpower him, he touched the socket of Jacob's hip so that his hip was wrenched as he wrestled with the man. Then the man said, "Let me go, for it is daybreak." But Jacob replied, "I will not let you go unless you bless me."*

The man asked him, "What is your name?"

"Jacob," he answered. Then the man said, "Your name will no longer be Jacob, but Israel, because you have struggled with God and with men and have overcome."

Jacob wouldn't let go until he received a blessing. Cling to God, wrestle with the angel and go the distance. There have been nights in my life that I have tossed and turned as I wrestled with life. There is nothing unholy about struggle. God is faithful to bless our efforts to make sense out of life. This is even true of strong followers of Jesus Christ. Faith must receive both nourishment and exercise.

What is involved in this type of intense faith? How can I become the person God wants me to be? How can we become the people God wants us to be? *"God is bigger than your questions,"* Ben would tell the kids who attended his youth group. Only after we dig in, dissect and examine something do we really understand and believe it.

Rational faith is more difficult than blind obedience; it is also stronger. When you struggle with a concept or a belief…asking why it's true…examining it from all different perspectives…you begin to buy more deeply into the belief or discard it. Then, and only then, do you move from blind agreement to a more pure faith based on logic led by the spirit of God. Questioning your beliefs is not the same as doubting your faith. God's love is stronger than our confusion or doubts or concerns or sadness. Nothing can prevent God from holding us tightly to himself while we struggle.

When I was teaching high school, I would challenge my students by explaining both sides of the issue. Many times, I would lead them to scriptures that were used as defense for opposing sides of an argument. They would look at me with puzzled expressions, *"Well? Then what is the correct answer?"* I would smile as I saw their mental wheels turning. I trusted their ability to... *"Do your best to present yourself to God as one approved, a workman who does not need to be ashamed and who correctly handles the word of truth." (2 Timothy 2:15)*

What they wanted were answers. I shuddered to hear those dreaded words, *"Will this be on the test?"* The test was not the point. The point was that they matured in faith; to develop strength and consistency in their lives. I would respond, in effect, *"My job is to give you the questions. Your responsibility is to figure out the answers. Go to the Bible. Talk with older, wiser Christians who can give you input. Discuss this with your families. Evaluate what you see in the media. Keep an open but discerning attitude. Maturing is not about memorizing answers. It is about learning how to think, process information and draw reasonable conclusions."* I wanted to teach them to think.

What would have happened if the followers of Jim Jones or David Koresh or Osama bin Ladin had used their minds instead of their passions? What about the travesty of children being molested by educational, religious or other leaders; could some of this have been avoided? We have an obligation to teach our children how to *think* as part of their faith. This is part of equipping people with truth through providing a safe place to question.

Questioning your faith is not easy. It takes work, research, study and prayer. It takes late night talks, long distance phone calls and lengthy emails to close friends. But it is worth it. We become stronger because we have challenged what we believe and we draw more closely to truth. We're able to handle the really tough things that life throws our way. To settle for less would be to short-change ourselves. Socrates put it this way, *"The unexamined life is not worth living."* That may be a bit of an overstatement but his point is well-taken.

Examine what you believe and why you believe it and you'll find that you become a stronger follower. But now comes the warning: be careful whom you choose as advisors. You know the bumper sticker that says, *"Don't follow me. I'm lost!"* This is excellent advice; don't try to find your answers from others who are also confused. You may find comfort but will likely legitimize a type of *collective ignorance.*

Go to people whose counsel you trust. Use the scripture as the ultimate authority. Maintain open relationships with others whose opinions you respect. Be willing to stretch and grow in safe environments. If you are sick, you do not go to the emergency room to seek the advice of other patients; you want to see a doctor. If you are struggling with the meaning of life, it doesn't make sense to join an on-line chat room or non-Christian support group or simply to complain with co-workers. This may set you up for greater grief because you are adding their confusion to your own. In contrast, find a mentor with the maturity to handle your questions without panic; one who is unafraid to struggle beside you.

"Now faith is being sure of what we hope for and certain of what we do not see." (Hebrews 11:1) There is a great deal of life we do not see. Faith is what keeps us moving; mature faith is what gives us the vision to keep moving forward.

Question everything. Depend on God to guide your steps.

◆   ◆   ◆

Where is he now? Ben Sharpton lives in Roswell, Georgia with his wife, Kay. They have two children, Nikki and Jonathon. Ben has earned two Masters degrees and has been a youth minister, training manager, and writer. Ben has contributed to over 130 magazine articles and book chapters in more than 30 different publications. He is the author of *"Everyday Issues and Fellowship Builders: Snap Sessions"*, and *"Service Heroes in Hospitality."*

Contentment with the status quo leads to stagnation. When we stop growing, we start dying; when we stop building, we start decaying; when we stop improving, we start worsening; when we stop gaining, we start losing; when we stop expanding, we start shrinking.

Charles W. Conn

o o o o o o o o o o o o o o o o o o o o o o o o o o o o o o o o

"The wise woman builds her house, but the foolish tears it down with her own hands. He who walks in his uprightness fears the LORD, but he who is devious in his ways despises Him."

—Proverbs 14:1-2 NASB

25

You become like the people
you hang around.

The people you've read about in these brief pages have a strong impact on my view of the world and understanding of faith. Somehow, being with them has made me more like Jesus. Their influence has been through the small tasks they approached as though great and noble; the huge tasks they handle with humility. I surround myself with quality people; not *powerful* or *rich* or *influential* or *impressive* but quality people of faith. This is my advice for you as well because the bottom line is, *you become like the people you hang around.* Each has influence in your life. A part of every close friend is imprinted on your soul when you truly connect. I have become a better person as a result of these and other friendships.

Jesus promised, *"For where two or three gather together because they are mine, I am there among them." (Matthew 18:20)* This is one of the most amazing promises in the Bible. This book is written for caring people. I allow myself to assume that you are a follower of our Lord although I recognize there are many deeply loving, caring people who are not Christians. If you are one of these people, then I simply thank you for your willingness to read these pages even when you were uncertain of the Christian perspective. There is a core experience in the Christian faith that when one gathers with other believers, the spirit of Jesus Christ is in their midst. *This gives me chills.* When Jesus was resurrected from the grave, he didn't die a second time; He is alive! Through his spirit, Jesus is actually with us when we share our lives with each other. We are not alone! The God of the Universe is here.

This is part of the reason why belonging to a body of believers is so vital. Christians should never operate as *Lone Rangers*. We are created for community. Find this in your local church with a whole bunch of other struggling people. Your presence there won't mess things up; they are not perfect people either. God makes it clear he wants us to gather and express our love for him. It is how we grow.

My wife says, *"Choose your friends wisely, and take care of those friendships."* Simple as that. A church building is not the only place to gather; experience authentic Christian community over a cup of coffee or soft-drink, or a meal, or a walk or a round of golf.

The Internet is not a place for intimacy; it is only an effective mode for communicating information.

Don't be misled into believing you are experiencing true community with people you never see. You may be able to keep up with friendships but cyber-world is wrought with dangers and illusions. God has created us to gather in person and share our lives. He carved in us a need for intimacy and authenticity through face-to-face relationships. We are created to breathe the same air as those we love.

Let me remind you of the importance of one-to-one time with young Christians and non-Christians. They become like you. It seems a great mystery how we get better just by getting together. The reason this is true is because Jesus is also there. He is the healer. We help each other get in touch with his presence. Somehow, we heal when we share. You are helping these folks heal by allowing them to share with you. This is a foundational belief of support groups and 12-step programs. It certainly needs to be promoted more often in the local church.

"To sum up, all of you be harmonious, sympathetic, brotherly, kind-hearted, and humble in spirit; not returning evil for evil or insult for insult,

but giving a blessing instead; for you were called for the very purpose that you might inherit a blessing." (1 Peter 3:8-9)

Don't just wait for people to come to church or place of ministry to learn about God's love. Go find them and share a heart full of love. They desperately need to experience the presence of the living God. This is the foundation for effective relational ministry. Ministry is a natural result of healthy relationships.

"So now I am giving you a new commandment: Love each other. Just as I have loved you, you should love each other. Your love for one another will prove to the world that you are my disciples." (John 13:34-35)

A few themes run through these pages...
Help others, ONLY in ways that make them stronger.
You learn a lot from people who may frighten you at first.
You'll probably get hurt along the way; get over it.
Relational ministry is about ministry relationships.
Always give but never be taken from.
Find the time to relax with your friends.
Don't worry about things before they happen.
Do what's right. Don't do what's wrong.
Build authentic relationships with other believers.
Reach out to non-believers on an individual basis.
Be true to yourself and don't forget to laugh.
Never take the junkies into your home.
Be careful. Pay attention.
Check your motives.
Oh, and don't forget...
You become like the people you hang around!
So, choose your friends wisely, and take care of those friendships.

"Don't worry about anything; instead, pray about everything. Tell God what you need, and thank him for all he has done. If you do this, you will experience God's peace, which is far more wonderful than the human mind can understand. His peace will guard your hearts and minds as you live in Christ Jesus. (Philippians 4:6-7)

Show me what road you follow and I will tell you what your
destination shall be; show me the companions you keep,
and I will tell you what sort of person you shall be.
Charles W. Conn

Discussion Guide for Small Group Studies

After participants read each chapter, use the following questions as a discussion guide. Discuss the scriptures. Conclude with, "How does this principle apply to your personal ministry?"

Chapter 1—If we switched chairs, this conversation would be different.

Tell about someone who made you feel good about yourself.

Do you notice the seating arrangement when you enter a room for a meeting? How does it feel to be in a disadvantaged position? What is the danger of vying for a position of power?

"The beginning of knowledge is recognizing that which we have not experienced; of knowing where we haven't been or cannot go." What does the author mean?

Do you agree with the statement that you are always a visitor in a cross-cultural ministry? Why or why not?

Scripture reference: Mark 10:42-44

Chapter 2—Show up. Show up, dressed. Show up, dressed and ready to play.

Have you ever learned something of value from someone when you didn't expect to? What is the danger in pre-judging someone?

Why is it important to "show up" for ministry? How does paying "attention to the details" of how we present ourselves important? Can you carry this too far? How?

Share about a time you showed up *ready to play*. How did it feel?

Scripture reference: Luke 14:28-29

Chapter 3—God is with you through the darkness.

When was the loneliest time in your life? Who helped you through it?

What other ways could Robin have reacted? How would you react?

Have you ever experienced this type of crisis? What helped you get through it? What would you say to someone in a similar situation?

Does this provide more comfort than to believe that God is in charge of all things, even tragedy?

Scripture references: John 8:12; John 14:1; John 14:27

Chapter 4—We'll try anything once.

What is the danger of being afraid to try? Is there anything you want to do but are afraid to try? Are you afraid of failure or success? What would you do if you knew you couldn't fail?

What is the new wine that the scripture refers to? What is the new wineskin? How does this apply to your ministry?

Are you attracted to ideas, just because they are new? How do you discern between impulsive risk-taking and leadership of the Spirit?

What are the steps for solving an old problem with a new approach?

Scripture references: Mark 2:22; Genesis 3:4-5; Matthew 25:14-30

Chapter 5—What will it matter in 100 years?

What tends to worry you? How do these worries affect your life? Do you know someone who makes *entertainment* out of worrying?

How would you describe *unconditional* love? What gives you the greatest assurance of God's love?

The author includes, "anger, resentment, grief, regret, guilt, lust, prejudice, hate, and pride" as feelings that rob your joy. How?

What are the things that will matter in 100 years?

Scripture references: Matthew 6:25-27, 31-34

Chapter 6—Sometimes you only have two choices, both wrong.

Think up some examples where you only have two wrong choices. Using these examples, come up with other possible options.

Why is it important to recognize the wrongness of a choice, even if you have to make it?

Has anyone ever sought your approval for an immoral choice? How did you respond? How do you think you would respond?

How do you "speak the truth in love" and maintain the friendship?

Scripture references: Ephesians 4:14-15; 1 John 1:8-10; Joshua 24:15.

Chapter 7—Never pet a wounded dog.

How can humor be used as a survival skill?

What are some ways you can be hurt by rushing into a situation too quickly? Share any experiences where this has happened.

Have you ever tried to "fix" someone? Have you ever experienced the "adrenaline rush" of helping people? Why is this dangerous?

What is most intimidating to you about relational ministry? What do you find the most rewarding?

Scripture reference: 1 Corinthians 8:6

Chapter 8—Consider the source.

Do you need to be liked by everyone? Does criticism bother you equally regardless of who gives it?

Does having Jesus Christ as your "boss" ever conflict with your other bosses in life? How do you resolve this conflict?

How is being "enamored by their cheers" and "intimidated by their jeers" connected? Have you ever experienced this from a group?

How do you handle feedback from others?

Scripture references: Luke 6:43-45; James 3:10-12; 2 Timothy 3:16-17; Colossians 1:15; John 15:18-20

Chapter 9—Your first ministry is to your family.

Discuss some positive examples of ministerial families. Why is it important for someone in the ministry to take care of his or her family?

What are some ways to minister to your family? How do these skills translate into ministry to others?

Ministry involves some level of sacrifice. How do you make sure you fulfill your calling and still take care of the needs of your family?

What changes could you make to have a better balanced life?

Scripture references: Ephesians 3:14-19

Chapter 10—First they appreciate it, then they expect it, then they're mad when you don't deliver.

Do you agree that people who belong to a minority ethnic group are generally more tuned-in to social interactions than the majority population? Why or why not?

Have you ever helped someone who became overly dependent on you? How did it end? What steps can you take to avoid being drawn in to these types of relationships?

Why would it be wise to avoid helping someone when they can take care of it themselves?

Scripture references: John 2:1-5; Matthew 10:16

Chapter 11—Watch out for blind triangles.

Come up with some examples of three people or organizations who you know have the potential of a blind triangle.

What makes these interactions negative? What are the dangers?

There are five examples as to why people create blind triangles. Discuss any other reasons you can think of why blind triangles occur.

What is your response when someone comes to you to complain about a third person? Avoid gossiping as you discuss your response.

Scripture references: Matthew 8:15-17; Luke 7:20-22; Matthew 5:37

Chapter 12—Never take the junkies into your home.

Have you ever known anyone who reminded you of Jabo? Discuss your feelings when you are interacting with this person.

Why is it important to keep the "junkies" out of your home? What are the dangers involved in letting them live with you?

How do you balance this advice with Matthew 25?

Do your priorities in ministry change when you have children? If so, how would your priorities be different? How might this advice create more sustainability and balance in ministry?

Scripture references: Matthew 25:35-40

Chapter 13—I'll never curse my God!

Jabo's lifestyle during his younger years may have contributed to his suffering later. Is this an important part of the story? Why?

How do you imagine his suffering may have helped him minister to others?

The author had never heard Jabo cry but was very familiar with the sound of his laugh. Why is this important?

Have you ever felt angry at God? How did you express this anger? Do you think Jabo had earned the right to address God in this way? Why was it important that he would never curse God?

Scripture reference: Job 29:11-17

Chapter 14—People are doing just about the best they can.

Do you basically believe in the sincerity of other people's efforts? How might you develop more patience with other people's flaws?

Are there areas in your life in which you need change? What seems to be the first step? How do you become more of the person Christ wants you to be?

What is the difference between conforming and transforming?

How is mental transformation connected with fulfilling God's will for us?

Scripture references: John 8:1-11; Romans 12:1-2

Chapter 15—If you don't have time to do it right the first time, when will you have time to go back and fix it?

Why was the relationship between these two brothers important when the older one corrected the younger one?

Do you ever struggle with representing Christ poorly? Where are the areas you are most tempted? Who holds you accountable?

Jesus acted immediately and gave his best in every situation. Give some other examples where this was true.

Why is it important for a Christian to bring excellence to every task?

Scripture references: Philippians 4:8; Luke 8:46-48; Ephesians 2:10

Chapter 16—I'm not on that committee.

Why is the ability to adapt an important part of effective ministry?

The author describes his "culture shock" and connects this with a desire to control his environment. Have you ever been in a similar situation?

Have you ever been drawn into a dispute that wasn't yours? Why is it good advice to pick and choose your battles wisely?

How does attitude about crisis affect our ability to face challenges?

Scripture references: 1 Corinthians 9:19-23

Chapter 17—Your greatest weakness, is your greatest strength, overdone.

Do you have anyone close to you who seems to be wired completely differently from you? Why is this a positive relationship?

What are your strengths? Share any experiences where they actually became a detriment by overdoing them.

The scripture says God chose "the weak things of the world to shame the strong." How does weakness help us mature in faith?

What is the danger in idolizing our own talents?

Scripture references: 1 Corinthians 1:26-31

Chapter 18—The way it is now is not the way it will always be.

Share a difficult experience you have been through. How did you have the courage to not give up?

Do you believe the quality of our lives is largely dependent on the choices we make? Why or why not?

Where are you struggling? Do you believe life will get better?

The scripture describes a process for developing hope. How do you see the difference between hope and wishful thinking?

How do you see God building character in your life?

Scripture references: Romans 5:1-5

Chapter 19—I just toss out words. It's your responsibility to put them together.

The opening section describes the power of words. How have you seen the power of words work in your life?

Do you sometimes obsess on getting it right? How can this become a "quasi-works" method of salvation?

Describe someone you know who always seems to be optimistic.

Is it difficult for you to think of Jesus as having a good sense of humor? Why or why not? How is positive humor an important aspect of relational ministry?

Scripture references: Luke 6:47-49; Luke 6:20-22

Chapter 20—We've got to understand this thing called Christian Community.

Describe your experience of authentic community.

Do you ever find yourself "wearing a mask" with your Christian friends? Why is it important to develop Christian community as a basis for relational ministry?

What part of the body do you represent? Use your imagination to describe how you fit into the body of Christ.

Do you tend to show your *best face* or your *worst possible self* (or somewhere in-between) when within your community of faith?

Scripture references: 1 Corinthians 12:12-19

Chapter 21—Love is a commitment.

Do you know a couple like Reuben and Marjorie, who seem to have deep, abiding commitment to their relationship? What are the elements that seem to be in place for such a relationship?

Describe your commitment to love those whom you serve in ministry.

Who are some of the "crowd of witnesses" in your life? How has their commitment to you strengthened your love for others?

"Feelings come and go..." What does this mean to you?

Scripture references: Hebrews 12:1-3; Galatians 6:2

Chapter 22—Those we serve are angels sent from God to teach us to fly.

Do you see those you help as messengers from God?

Why is it important to have this level of respect for those you serve? What does the scriptural reference, "as if you yourselves were suffering" mean to you?

Have you ever asked for help and felt resentment? How did it feel? Have you resented people you have helped?

Tell about a time you saw someone showing favoritism. Why do you think James is so direct on this point?

Scripture references: Hebrews 13:1-3; James 2:5-9

Chapter 23—The glass is half empty. The glass is half full. I say, 'Get a new glass!'

Describe someone you know who has risen above their circumstances and maintained a positive attitude about life.

Do you tend to make excuses? How can you change this tendency?

Why is it important to recognize weaknesses but not define yourself by them?

At what point should a Christian seek counseling?

Scripture references: 2 Corinthians 5:17-21

Chapter 24—Question everything.

Why is it important to examine your faith?

Where do you look for the answers? What if you do not find an answer to your question?

What are the dangers in the "unexamined" life? Is it possible to over-examine your life? How do we find balance?

How does having a well developed faith help you minister to others? What is the danger in not having an examined faith in ministry situations?

Scripture references: James 1:2-4; Genesis 32:22-32; Philippians 2:12; Hebrews 11:1

Chapter 25—You become like the people you hang around.

Who do you hang around that helps you become more like Jesus?

Why is it important to have good friends? Who are some of the people who have influenced you the most?

Have you ever tried being a "Lone Ranger" Christian? Did it work for you? What are the dangers faced with this attitude?

Who are you reaching out to with the love of Christ? How are you reaching out to them? Can you see a change in them? How can you reach out to non-Christians without being negatively influenced? How are you growing in your love for others?

Scripture references: Matthew 18:20; 1 Peter 3:8-9; John 13:34-35; Philippians 4:6-7

Books by Dr. Charles W. Conn can be ordered on-line at
www.pathwaybookstore.com

About the Author

Bob Ayres is a husband, father, friend, minister, educator, and writer who lives in Louisville, Kentucky with his wife, Kathy and their children, Christina, David, Casey, John and Ana. Bob grew up in Florida and still sports a *Gators* tag on the front of the family van. He graduated from the University of Florida in Gainesville, Florida with a Bachelor of Arts in Education, Southern Baptist Theological Seminary in Louisville with a Master of Religious Education and Brenau University in Gainesville, Georgia with a Master of Education. He continues to ponder about a doctoral program but has to wait in line for family educational funding.

Bob has skills for bringing people together around common missions. He has used these strengths for the development of non-profit and ministry organizations for the purpose of helping others physically, emotionally, intellectually, relationally, and spiritually. He has led in establishing various programs and organizations over the years. He has a unique ability to understand a need, creatively conceptualize a solution, design an effective strategy for meeting this need, and implementing the appropriate program or idea.

Bob and Kathy are the founders of a national outreach ministry for Deaf and Hard-of-Hearing teenagers called DeafYouth Ministries. The program name for the local ministries is *DTQuest* which is a shortened form of Deaf Teen Quest. *DTQuest* is most similar to *Young Life* or *Youth For Christ* for Deaf teenagers. More can be learned about the ministry of DTQuest at the website, *www.dtquest.org*

You can also find a list of other books by Bob Ayres at *www.bobayres.com*

0-595-32595-5